PASSING THE GEORGIA EOCT

IN

ECONOMICS

Kindred Howard
Katie Herman

Edited by Devin Pintozzi

American Book Company
PO Box 2638
Woodstock, GA 30188-1383
Toll Free: 1 (888) 264-5877   Phone: (770) 928-2834
Toll Free Fax: 1 (866) 827-3240
Web site: www.americanbookcompany.com

ACKNOWLEDGEMENTS

The authors would like to gratefully acknowledge the editing and technical contributions of Marsha Torrens and Yvonne Benson.

We also want to thank Charisse Johnson her expertise in developing the graphics for this book.

This product/publication includes images from CorelDRAW 9 and 11 which are protected by the copyright laws of the United States, Canada, and elsewhere. Used under license.

Table of Contents

Chapter 3 Macroeconomic Concepts 55

Chapter 4 The International Economy 73

PREFACE

Passing the Georgia End of Course Test in Economics will help students who are learning or reviewing material for the EOC Test. The materials in this book are based on the testing standards as published by the Georgia Department of Education.

This book contains several sections. These sections are as follows: 1) General information about the book; 2) A Diagnostic Test; 3) An Evaluation Chart; 4) Chapters that teach the concepts and skills that improve graduation readiness; 5) Two Practice Tests. Answers to the tests and exercises are in a separate manual. The answer manual also contains a Chart of Standards for teachers to make a more precise diagnosis of student needs and assignments.

We welcome comments and suggestions about the book. Please contact us at

American Book Company
PO Box 2638
Woodstock, GA 30188-1383

Toll Free: 1 (888) 264-5877
Phone: (770) 928-2834
Fax: (770) 928-7483
Web site: www.americanbookcompany.com

ABOUT THE AUTHORS

Kindred Howard is a 1991 alumnus of the University of North Carolina at Chapel Hill, where he graduated with a B.S. in Criminal Justice and national honors in Political Science. In addition to two years as a probation & parole officer in North Carolina, he has served for over twelve years as a teacher and writer in the fields of religion and social studies. His experience includes teaching students at both the college and high school level, as well as speaking at numerous seminars and authoring several books on US history, American government, and economics. Mr. Howard is currently completing both a M.A. in history from Georgia State University and a M.A. in biblical studies from Asbury Theological Seminary. In addition to serving as Social Studies Coordinator for American Book Company, Mr. Howard is the president/CEO of KB Howard Writing, Consulting, and Administrative Services and lives in Kennesaw, Georgia, with his wife and three children.

Katie Herman is a senior at Kennesaw State University and will graduate in May 2008 with a Bachelor's degree in English. Her experience includes working as a writing tutor and editor at the collegiate level, as well as authoring several academic essays. After graduation, she plans to pursue a M.A. in professional writing. Ms. Herman currently lives in Woodstock, Georgia.

TEST-TAKING TIPS

1. Complete the chapters and practice tests in this book. This text will help you review the skills for English/Language Arts: Reading. The book also contains materials for reviewing skills under the Research standards.

2. Be prepared. Get a good night's sleep the day before your exam. Eat a well-balanced meal, one that contains plenty of proteins and carbohydrates, prior to your exam.

3. Arrive early. Allow yourself at least 15–20 minutes to find your room and get settled. Then you can relax before the exam, so you won't feel rushed.

4. Think success. Keep your thoughts positive. Turn negative thoughts into positive ones. Tell yourself you will do well on the exam.

5. Practice relaxation techniques. Some students become overly worried about exams. Before or during the test, they may perspire heavily, experience an upset stomach, or have shortness of breath. If you feel any of these symptoms, talk to a close friend or see a counselor. They will suggest ways to deal with test anxiety. Here are some quick ways to relieve test anxiety:

   • Imagine yourself in your most favorite place. Let yourself sit there and relax.

   • Do a body scan. Tense and relax each part of your body starting with your toes and ending with your forehead.

   • Use the 3-12-6 method of relaxation when you feel stress. Inhale slowly for 3 seconds. Hold your breath for 12 seconds, and then exhale slowly for 6 seconds.

6. Read directions carefully. If you don't understand them, ask the proctor for further explanation before the exam starts.

7. Use your best approach for answering the questions. Some test-takers like to skim the questions and answers before reading the problem or passage. Others prefer to work the problem or read the passage before looking at the answers. Decide which approach works best for you.

8. Answer each question on the exam. Unless you are instructed not to, make sure you answer every question. If you are not sure of an answer, take an educated guess. Eliminate choices that are definitely wrong, and then choose from the remaining answers.

9. Use your answer sheet correctly. Make sure the number on your question matches the number on your answer sheet. In this way, you will record your answers correctly. If you need to change your answer, erase it completely. Smudges or stray marks may affect the grading of your exams, particularly if they are scored by a computer. If your answers are on a computerized grading sheet, make sure the answers are dark. The computerized scanner may skip over answers that are too light.

10. Check your answers. Review your exam to make sure you have chosen the best responses. Change answers only if you are sure they are wrong.

Georgia US Economics
Diagnostic Test

The purpose of this diagnostic test is to measure your knowledge in US economics. This test is based on the GPS-based EOCT standards for US economics and adheres to the sample question format provided by the Georgia Department of Education.

General Directions:

1. Read all directions carefully.

2. Read each question or sample. Then choose the best answer.

3. Choose only one answer for each question. If you change an answer, be sure to erase your original answer completely.

4. After taking the test, you or your instructor should score it using the evaluation chart following the test. This will enable you to determine your strengths and weaknesses. Then, study chapters in this book corresponding to topics that you need to review.

1   Misha likes the law and is attempting to decide between a career as a lawyer, a police officer, or a paralegal. As a lawyer, Misha can expect to earn $120,000 a year working 50 hours a week, but he will have to forgo six years of income while he is in school. As a paralegal, Misha will earn $37,000 a year working 40 hours per week Monday through Friday, but he will only be able to work part-time, low-income jobs for the two years he will be in school. As a police officer, Misha will earn $45,000 a year working about 40 hours a week- though his schedule will be irregular and his job more dangerous, but he can get his education on the job. Misha decides to be a lawyer, which of the following can be seen as an opportunity cost of this decision?   EF1

A   smaller income
B   irregular schedule
C   loss of income in the immediate future
D   There is no opportunity cost because he will earn more money.

2   With respect to the circular flow model, businesses provide households with which of the following.   MI1

A   taxes and interest
B   labor and taxes
C   goods, services, and incomes
D   public goods and transfer payments

3   Juan goes to the Southern Union Bank to get a loan. Juan has an account at the bank on which he receives 2.2% annual interest. Which of the following can be said of the rate of interest he will pay on the loan that he takes out?   PF2

A   It will be lower than 2.2%
B   Nothing can be known about it, because he has not yet applied.
C   It will be higher than 2.2%
D   It will be lower than 2.2%

4   The Federal Reserve System is concerned that the US economy might be on the verge of a deflationary period much like the one suffered by the Japanese. Which of the following actions might the Fed take together that will both increase the money supply?   MA2

A   open market sales, decreasing the discount rate
B   increasing the reserve requirement, decreasing the discount rate
C   open market purchases, increase the reserve requirement
D   open market purchases, decreasing the reserve requirement

5   Myra Worthington, CEO of CompuGlobal Corp., complains that the company's software products have a very high price elasticity of demand. What is Myra saying?   MI3

A   The higher the demand for her product, the lower its price.
B   Small changes in price result in large changes in quantity demanded.
C   No matter what the price, people want the same quantity of her product.
D   Consumers don't want her product if she lowers the price too much.

6 Below is a "supply & demand" schedule that shows the number of pairs of socks that producers are willing to make at various prices, as well as the number of pairs that consumers are willing to purchase at each price. Using this chart, what would happen if the price of the socks was set at $2.50/pair? `MI2`

Price	Produced	Demanded
$0.50	0	1,000
$1.00	100	900
$1.50	200	800
$2.00	300	700
$2.50	400	600
$3.00	500	500
$3.50	600	400
$4.00	700	300
$4.50	800	200
$5.00	900	100
$5.50	1,000	0

A All socks would sell because it would be the equilibrium price.

B a shortage

C a surplus

D No socks would be produced because it would be the equilibrium price.

7 Using the same chart, what would happen if producers raised the price to $3.50/pair? `MI2`

A The socks would be priced at the equilibrium price.

B No one would buy socks because they are priced too high.

C a surplus

D a shortage

8 The new chairman of the National Council of Economic Advisors believes that there is a great risk imposed by US trade deficits. Which of the following recommendations might the chairman make to reduce the trade deficit? `IN3`

A Increase the exchange value of the dollar.

B Decrease tariffs and quotas on foreign products.

C Increase interest rates.

D Devalue the dollar.

9 Typesetters were once responsible for placing strings of individual letters in place on a plate to print books and newspapers. In the 20th century, this position was completely eliminated by developments in computer and printing press technology. What type of unemployment does this represent? `MA1`

A cyclical

B frictional

C structural

D seasonal

10 Which of the following statements BEST explains why governments typically own and maintain parks? `EF5`

A It is a job which is too big for business firms to carry out.

B People do not trust private businesses with such an important task.

C Governments need to perform such tasks to justify taxation.

D Parks would not otherwise be produced in the quantity desired.

GO ON

11 Ted wants to be a doctor. He also _{PF1} wants to buy a brand new car. Since both medical school and the new car arc vcry expensive, Ted cannot afford to do both. If Ted decides that the benefits of going to medical school will ultimately outweigh the gratification of buying a new car, then the MOST rational thing Ted could do is

A use the money for medical school.

B invest the money in bonds.

C buy the car.

D avoid using the car as a trade-off.

12 Sophie is the major income _{PF5} earner for her family. For this reason, Sophie is concerned that her family would struggle financially if she got hurt and could not work, or even worse, died and was no longer around. Sophie asks you what steps she could take to ease some of her concerns. The BEST answer you could give her is to tell her to

A invest in liability insurance.

B invest in promising stocks.

C invest in life and disability insurance.

D invest in health and life insurance.

13 The US income tax charges _{PF3} higher rates for those with higher incomes. Wealthy individuals are said to be in higher tax brackets and poorer people in lower tax brackets. This is an example of

A a regressive tax.

B a progressive tax.

C a proportional tax.

D a user fee.

14 A volcano erupts in Hawaii that _{MI2} destroys or damages many of the orchards that supply the US with pineapples. What will be the effect on price and quantity of pineapples sold, assuming all else is equal?

A Price will rise and quantity will also rise.

B Price will drop and quantity will also drop.

C Price will drop but quantity will rise.

D Price will rise but quantity will drop.

15 Frank owns his own printing _{EF2} firm. Since business has been going well, he wants to look at ways he can increase production. After assessing his resources and potential business, he determines that hiring two new employees and buying a new printing press will enable him to increase his production by 20% over a four-month period. Therefore, Frank hires the two employees and purchases the press. Frank's actions are a perfect example of a/an

A opportunity cost.

B trade-off.

C rational economic decision.

D trade barrier.

16 Which of the following economic _{IN2} actors is MOST LIKELY to support free trade?

A the United Steelworkers of America

B Coca-Cola™ Corporation

C the Anti-Globalization Coalition

D US electronics producers

17 The graph below shows the number of US dollars that one Euro will buy IN3
for the period from 2003 to early 2005. Which of the following statements
BEST describes the general trend of the US dollar exchange rate against the
Euro?

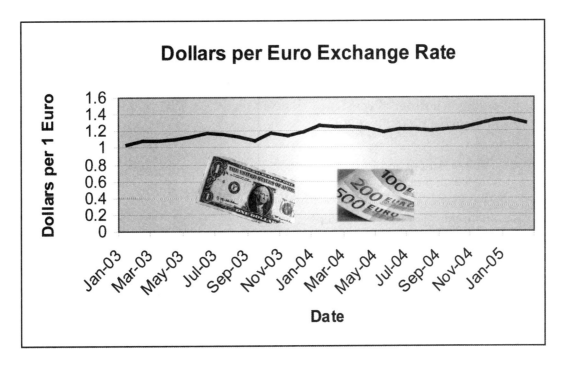

A The US dollar is depreciating against the Euro.

B The US dollar is appreciating against the Euro.

C This graph only tells the Euro exchange against the dollar. One cannot tell what
the dollar exchange against the Euro is doing.

D The US dollar is completely stable against the Euro.

18 On which of the following loans PF4
would one be MOST LIKELY to
pay the highest interest rate?

   A a home mortgage loan

   B an automobile loan

   C a credit card

   D a student loan for college

19 The IRS lays off thousands of MA1
employees every year after
April 15th (the deadline for citizens
to file tax returns). This is an example
of

   A seasonal unemployment.

   B cyclical unemployment.

   C frictional unemployment.

   D structural unemployment.

GO ON

20 Which of the following describes how goods pass from producers to consumers in a free enterprise system?   EF3

   A   capital investment

   B   voluntary exchange

   C   consumer sovereignty

   D   taxes and subsidies

21 What can one assume from the following headline: "President and Congress Feud Over Fiscal Policy"?   MA3

   A   The president and Congress cannot agree on a tax plan and/or a budget.

   B   The president favors higher taxes but Congress opposes them.

   C   Congress and the president cannot agree on defense spending.

   D   Congress and the president cannot agree on interest rates.

22 In a market economy, which of the following laws would one be MOST LIKELY to find implemented by the government?   EF4

   A   laws that set the price of fruits and vegetables

   B   laws instructing firms of how many workers to employ

   C   laws requiring all property unsold after 90 days to be given to the government

   D   laws preventing individuals from destroying the property of others

23 The use of money in an economy solves which of the following problems?   MI1

   A   scarcity

   B   the condition of opportunity cost

   C   an efficient means of economic exchange

   D   trade barriers

24 Which of the following people will LIKELY find the highest paying job in the workforce?   PF6

   A   someone with a high school diploma

   B   someone with a college degree and additional training

   C   someone with mediocre communication skills

   D   someone with a history of bouncing from job to job.

25 With respect to raising funds, the primary difference between a corporation and other types of businesses is that   MI4

   A   they can sell shares of the company to the general public.

   B   they obtain loans from banks.

   C   they always have collateral, but other businesses do not.

   D   they can more easily make decisions about whether to seek a loan.

26 The government of Bugonia will spend $13 million more this year than it receives in revenue. Which of the following statements can be made with certainty?   MA1

   A   Bugonia's debt is growing.

   B   Bugonia is experiencing a budget deficit.

   C   Bugonia will experience a trade deficit.

   D   Bugonia will experience a trade surplus.

27 Congress approves a budget that allocates how much money will be spent on defense, education, social programs, etc. Their plan also calls for an increase in taxes to help pay for all the expenses. This plan defines what? MA3

A   the government's monetary policy

B   the government's fiscal policy

C   the government's revenue

D   the government's reserve requirement

28 Igor Petrovich is a Russian businessman who does a great deal of business in Serbia. Currently one Russian ruble (currency) will buy 2.2 Serbian dinars (currency.) Igor is attempting to decide whether to buy a new suit of clothes in Moscow (Russia) or Belgrade (Serbia.) If the exchange rate just changed to one ruble per 2.75 dinars, where should he buy the suit and why? IN3

A   in Serbia because the ruble has appreciated

B   in Russia because the ruble has depreciated

C   in Serbia because the ruble has depreciated

D   in Russia because the ruble has appreciated

29 Which of the following is a MONETARY policy that might be used to reduce inflation? MA2

A   decreasing taxation

B   decreasing the discount rate

C   open market sales

D   increasing government spending

30 MagnaFlare is a corporation that makes road flares. One of the primary components of MagnaFlare's flares is ground magnesium. How would the magnesium ore, from which ground magnesium is made, be classified as a factor of production? EF1

A   capital

B   land

C   entrepreneurship

D   It is not a factor of production, it is a product.

31 On a supply and demand diagram, if the demand curve shifts to the left, which of the following will happen to the equilibrium price and quantity? MI2

A   Both price and quantity will rise.

B   Both price and quantity will decline.

C   Price will rise and quantity will decline.

D   Price will decline and quantity will rise.

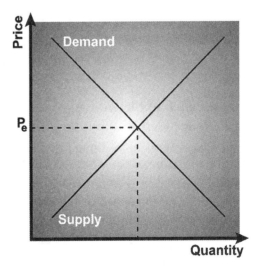

GO ON

32 To say that net exports is nega-   IN1
tive is the same as saying that

   A   there is a capital account deficit.

   B   there is a budget deficit.

   C   the exchange rate has depreciated.

   D   there is a current account deficit.

Look at the production possibilities curve below and answer the following question.

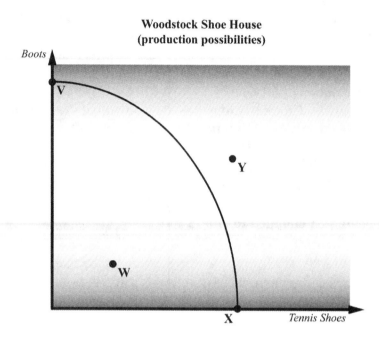

Woodstock Shoe House
(production possibilities)

33 At which point on the curve would Woodstock Shoe House be failing to   EF2
produce either product efficiently?

   A V   **B** W   **C** X   **D** Y

34 Which of the following is least   EF6
associated with human capital?

   A   medical treatment that reduces time off of work due to illness or injury

   B   maintenance of fully-automated production facilities

   C   a college course in accounting

   D   an on-the-job training course in the latest production methods

35 Kelly works for a large law firm   PF1
in San Diego. Her boss informs
her that a promotion will be available
in the next 4 months. Kelly wants the
job, so she works as hard as she can
to impress her boss and bring in profits for the company. Kelly is motivated by a

   A   negative incentive.

   B   positive incentive.

   C   rational decision.

   D   list of alternatives.

36 The US and Canada have been experiencing a conflict over US restrictions on imported softwood lumber. Which of the following groups would be MOST LIKELY to support the US restrictions? _IN2_

A   Canadian lumber firms

B   US new home buyers

C   US lumber importers

D   US lumber firms

37 Arthur gets his 2006 tax returns back from his accountant to discover that he owes fewer taxes this year than last year. As a result, he gets a refund check for $3000. What impact will this have on Arthur? _PF3_

A   He will be more likely to spend money on consumer goods and services.

B   He will be less likely to spend money on consumer goods and services.

C   He will not have to depend as heavily on subsidies as he did the previous year.

D   He will pay fewer tariffs.

38 Annabelle is tired of making less than $40,000 a year. Which of the following is the BEST way for Annabelle to raise her earning potential? _PF6_

A   Support subsidies that will protect US jobs.

B   Save more of her income.

C   Invest in capital.

D   Acquire more education and training.

39 Senator Harksten fears that flower growers in his state will not be able to afford to stay in business given the low price for tulips. He proposes that a minimum price be established for tulips that is above the current equilibrium price. Which of the following would BEST describe this law and its effect? _EF5_

A   It is a price ceiling that will cause a surplus.

B   It is a price floor that will cause a surplus.

C   It is a price ceiling that will cause a shortage.

D   It is a price floor that will cause a shortage.

40 Which of the following would one expect to find in a command economy? _EF4_

A   a government product planning commission

B   a lack of government intervention in the economy

C   strict protection of private property rights

D   underproduction of public goods

41 The Consumer Price Index (CPI) is an indicator of which of the following? _MA1_

A.   the size of an economy

B.   the velocity of money

C.   the level of inflation or deflation

D.   the presence of a budget deficit or surplus

Diagnostic Test   Session II   Do not begin until your teacher tells you to.

42 How did the invention of money change early economic systems? MI1

- A It changed what goods people needed.
- B It changed how goods were produced.
- C It provided a medium of exchange that made transactions easier.
- D It created the concept of debt.

43 A market that has few barriers to entry, in which products that are not of identical quality and style are sold, and, therefore, firms can make greater than normal profits for short periods of time is BEST described as MI4

- A monopolistic.
- B oligopolistic.
- C perfectly competitive.
- D monopolistically competitive.

44 Many in the US government are concerned about the depreciation of the US dollar. Such individuals would like to increase the value of the dollar. Which of the following presents the BEST argument for or against whether the value of the dollar should be increased? IN3

- A Yes, boosting the value of the dollar will increase US exports.
- B Yes, boosting the dollar will decrease US imports.
- C No, boosting the dollar will anger foreign consumers and start a trade war.
- D No, boosting the dollar will increase US imports and decrease US exports.

45 Which of the following statements provides the BEST definition of economics? EF1

- A the study of money
- B the study of how businesses operate
- C the study of why people behave and make decisions in the manner they do
- D the study of how scarce resources are allocated to attain wants

46 A breakthrough in nanotechnology allows silicon chips for computers to be produced much more quickly and cheaply. If demand for computers remains unchanged, what will be the effect upon market price and supply? [Hint: draw a supply and demand diagram, if necessary.] MI2

- A Both price and supply will rise.
- B Both price and supply will fall.
- C The supply will rise while the price falls.
- D The supply will fall while the price rises.

47 Which of the following is one of the tasks conducted by the Federal Reserve System? MA2

- A executing fiscal policy
- B printing money
- C preparing the budget of the federal government
- D making loans to commercial banks

48 The graph below shows the US balance of trade in goods and services, as   IN1
    well as the value of US exports in goods and services. Which of the follow-
    ing can be concluded from this graph?

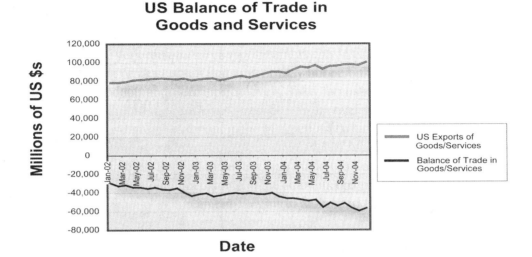

A   The graph must be wrong because exports are climbing, so the balance of trade
     cannot possibly be falling.

B   The US must be investing more in foreign countries than they are investing in
     the US.

C   US imports must be greater than US exports and rising at a faster rate.

D   The US must be experiencing a recession during the period shown on the
     graph.

49 Japan claims that the snow in   IN2
    Japan is different from that
    experienced elsewhere. Because of
    this, the country of Japan has pro-
    duced laws which prevent skis from
    being imported into the country
    unless they meet certain specifica-
    tions. Which of the following terms
    might describe this type of law?

A   tariff
B   quota
C   standard based trade barrier
D   non-trade related restriction

50 GDP, CPI, the unemployment   MA1
    rate, and the national debt are
    all what?

A   signs that the economy is peaking
B   signs that the economy is in con-
     traction
C   economic indicators used to deter-
     mine the state and direction of the
     economy
D   the result of economic expansion

GO ON

51 In England, the government owns industries such as the airline, TV stations, hospitals, universities, and defense contractors. However, most other industries involve privately owned firms that compete for business. Which of the following would BEST describe the type of economy England has? _EF4_

- **A** traditional
- **B** command
- **C** market
- **D** mixed

52 Under which of the following circumstances might a country devalue its currency? _IN3_

- **A** The country is running high trade srpluses.
- **B** The country is running high current account surpluses.
- **C** The country is running high trade deficits.
- **D** The country is running high budget deficits.

53 All of the following are characteristics of perfectly competitive markets EXCEPT _MI4_

- **A** firm's prices are kept confidential.
- **B** production is similar in quality.
- **C** there are a large number of buyers and sellers.
- **D** there are few barriers to entering the market.

54 DVD players are purchased by consumers in what kind of market? _MI2_

- **A** product market
- **B** social market
- **C** factor market
- **D** mixed market

55 Japan and South Korea make cars and TVs. The amount of each item that each country can make in one hour can be seen in the following table. Which of the strategies listed below would create a situation in which there were more of both products? _IN1_

	Televisions	Automobiles
South Korea	100	5
Japan	200	100

- **A** South Korea makes all of the TV sets, and Japan makes all the cars.
- **B** South Korea makes all of the cars, and Japan makes all the TV sets.
- **C** South Korea makes all TV sets, and Japan gives up 50 TV sets in favor of 25 cars.
- **D** Japan makes all of the cars, and South Korea shifts half of its car production to TVs.

56 Tony is about to travel to England on business. While he is there, he hopes to see some of the sites and dine at some fine restaurants. In order to know how much money he should budget, Tony needs to know how many British pounds his US dollars are worth. Tony needs to be aware of what? _IN3_

- **A** the exchange rate
- **B** any current embargoes
- **C** international tariffs
- **D** whether or not the US dollar currently enjoys a comparative advantage in trade

57 Donald works as an accountant for a large corporation. Which of the following terms would BEST describe his role? _EF1_

- **A** entrepreneur
- **C** laborer
- **B** firm
- **D** consumer

58 Due to inflation, the Federal Reserve decides to decrease the money supply. Which one of the following will the Federal Reserve MOST LIKELY do? *MA2*

   A   Lower the discount rate.

   B   Implement an "easy money" policy.

   C   Buy bonds.

   D   Raise the reserve requirement for banks.

59 Nations that are the target of embargoes are forced to deal with which of the following? *IN2*

   A   increased scarcity

   B   falling prices

   C   lower tariffs

   D   more foreign competition

60 Saying that net exports are positive is the same as saying that— *MA1*

   A   There is a current account surplus.

   B   There is a capital account surplus.

   C   There is a current account deficit.

   D   The same weight of goods has been imported as were exported.

61 A pair of shoes that costs $80 last month costs $100 this month. Which of the following BEST describes this economic condition? *MA1*

   A   inflation

   B   recession

   C   stagflation

   D   competition

62 Which of the following is associated with a command economy? *EF4*

   A   full employment

   B   private property

   C   inventions

   D   innovations

63 Brian wants to buy a soda and a box of popcorn at the movies. However, he only has enough money for one or the other. If Brian buys the soda, which of the following is his "opportunity cost"? *EF1*

   A   the price of the soda

   B   the price of the popcorn

   C   the satisfaction of eating the popcorn

   D   his thirst

64 In 2007, the United States experienced record numbers of home foreclosures. In other words, because many people had signed home loans that they ultimately could not afford to pay back, record numbers lost their homes to lenders. Lenders were able to take these homes because the homes were *PF5*

   A   illegally bought.

   B   uninsured.

   C   collateral.

   D   part of a housing surplus.

65 The way the government conducts spending and taxation is called what? *MA3*

   A   monetary policy

   B   economic policy

   C   free enterprise policy

   D   fiscal policy

66 A market structure in which only one producer supplies a good that is in demand, thereby permitting them to set the price by how much they supply, is called what? *MI4*

   A   competition

   B   monopoly

   C   oligopoly

   D   conglomerate

67 The way the government chooses to control the money supply is called what?   MA2

   A   monetary policy

   B   open market operation

   C   reserve requirement and discount rate

   D   fiscal policy

68 Bauxite, the ore used to make aluminum, would be considered among which of the following factors of production?   EF1

   A   capital

   B   land

   C   labor

   D   entrepreneurship

69 Economic system based on equity and in which the government decides what gets made and sets prices is called what?   EF4

   A   market system

   B   traditional economy

   C   political economy

   D   command economy

70 Which of the following might be a sign of economic trough?   MA1

   A   low unemployment

   B   recession

   C   high GDP

   D   stable CPI

71 The study of how individuals, firms, and nations can BEST allocate their limited resources is called what?   EF1

   A   entrepreneurship

   B   economics

   C   study of production

   D   capital

72 George has just saved enough money to buy the car he's dreamed of. He puts down $5000 in cash and finances the rest through his local credit union. George's car is what?   MI1

   A   a consumer good

   B   a capital good

   C   a production cost

   D   a renewable resource

73 What are the four types of economic systems?   EF4

   A   production, market, command, free

   B   market, traditional, mixed, command

   C   command, labor, capital, traditional

   D   free, command, communist, mixed

74 What are the three major economic actors in the US economy?   MI1

   A   government, the market, entrepreneurs

   B   land, capital, labor

   C   households, businesses, government

   D   consumers, producers, businesses

75 The price at which total supply equals total demand is known as what?

   A   the middle price

   B   the consumer price

   C   consumer demand

   D   the equilibrium price

76 Jordan works for the state of Georgia as a probation officer. His labor provides the government with a much needed service. In return, the state pays Jordan a salary. With his salary, Jordan purchases the goods he needs/wants from private firms. He also pays taxes that allow the government to continue to provide protection and government services. Jordan's economic interdependence with the government and private businesses is referred to as what? `MI1`

A   the money flow
B   the monetary cycle
C   circular flow of economic activity
D   economic independence

77 NAFTA BEST represents the controversy that exists over `IN2`

A   scarcity.
B   embargoes.
C   debt.
D   trade barriers.

78 Fiscal policy is MOST influenced by `IN23`

A   Congress.
B   the "Fed."
C   the federal board of governors.
D   businesses.

79 Linwood and Sylvia both go to the store to buy the latest iPod®. They both pay the same amount for the product. However, because Sylvia earns less money than Linwood, she actually ends up paying a higher percentage of her income than Linwood does in sales tax. Such a tax is called `PF3`

A   progressive.
B   regressive.
C   proportional.
D   illegal.

80 Paul wants to buy a classic sports car. Unfortunately, only a limited amount of dealers and collectors have the model car he wants. As a result, Paul will have to pay a high price, if he can even get the car at all. Paul is experiencing what? `EF1`

A   an embargo on cars
B   severe inflation
C   scarcity
D   depression in the car market

EVALUATION CHART FOR GEORGIA GPS ECONOMICS DIAGNOSTIC TEST

Directions: On the following chart, circle the question numbers that you answered incorrectly, and evaluate the results. These questions are based on the *standards and benchmarks published by the Georgia Department of Education.* Then turn to the appropriate chapters, read the explanations, and complete the exercises. Review other chapters as needed. Finally, complete the Practice test(s) to assess your progress and further prepare you for the **Georgia End of Course Test in Economics**.

Note: Some question numbers may appear under multiple chapters because those questions require demonstration of multiple skills.

Chapter	Diagnostic Test Question(s)
Chapter 1: Fundamental Economic Concepts	1, 10, 15, 20, 22, 30, 33, 34, 39, 40, 45, 51, 62, 63, 68 69, 71, 73, 80
Chapter 2: Concepts	2, 5, 6, 7, 14, 23, 25, 31, 42, 43, 46, 53, 54, 66, 72, 74, 75, 76
Chapter 3: Macroeconomic Concepts	4, 9, 19, 21, 26, 27, 29, 41, 47, 50, 58, 60, 61, 65, 67, 70
Chapter 4: The International Economy	16, 17, 28, 32, 36, 44, 49, 48, 52, 55, 56, 59, 77, 78
Chapter 5: Personal Finance Economics	3, 11, 12, 13, 18, 24, 35, 37, 38, 64, 79

Chapter 1
Fundamental Economic Concepts

SSEF1	The student will explain why limited productive resources and unlimited wants result in scarcity, opportunity costs, and trade-offs for individuals, businesses, and governments.
SSEF2	The student will give examples of how rational decision making entails comparing the marginal benefits and the marginal costs of an action.
SSEF3	The student will explain how specialization and voluntary exchange between buyers and sellers increase the satisfaction of both parties.
SSEF4	The student will compare and contrast different economic systems and explain how they answer the three basic economic questions of what to produce, how to produce, and for whom to produce.
SSEF5	The student will describe the roles of government in a market economy.
SSEF6	The student will explain how productivity, economic growth, and future standards of living are influenced by investment in factories, machinery, new technology, and the health, education, and training of people.

1.1 RESOURCES AND WANTS

Economics is the study of how individuals, businesses (sometimes referred to as *firms*), and nations can best allocate their limited resources. In other words, how can people get the most benefit out of the limited resources available and at the lowest cost. **Wants** may be things people must have to live (food, shelter, clothing, etc.), or simply goods and services one desires and would obtain if he/she could. While wants might be unlimited, resources for obtaining them (i.e., money) are not. Therefore, people, businesses, and even governments have to make choices about how to spend their resources. This is why we study economics.

RESOURCES

Resources are defined as those things which humans can put to productive use. Resources include money, people (particularly their labor), time, information, machines, and natural resources. *Natural resources* are all of the raw materials in nature used to produce what humans need or want (timber, water, iron ore, crude oil, natural gas, coal, fish, uranium, and arable [farmable] land). There are two kinds of natural resources: *renewable* and *nonrenewable*. A renewable natural resource is a resource that can be replenished (replaced) over time. A good example of a

Natural Resources

renewable natural resource is timber. We cut trees down to make furniture, decks, baseball bats, paper, and so on. However, we can plant more trees and replenish the supply for future use. A nonrenewable natural resource, on the other hand, is a natural resource that cannot be replenished over time. An important example of a nonrenewable natural resource is petroleum (crude oil). It takes millions of years for petroleum to form, so there is a fixed supply of petroleum under the ground. When it is gone, there will be no more. It is important to remember that even renewable natural resources can be expended if they aren't given a chance to renew.

PRODUCTIVE RESOURCES

Corporation

Most resources need to be properly processed in order to produce things that are needed and/or wanted. There are **four basic productive resources (factors of production)**: *land, labor, capital,* and *entrepreneurship*. These four factors are elements of virtually any business, whether it is a small gift shop or a massive multinational corporation.

When economists use the term *land*, they use it in a much broader sense than most people. **Land** includes not only the property on which a production plant is built, but also all other natural resources involved. So remember, in terms of economics, "land" is more than the ground you stand on. Land includes any timber, water, iron ore, crude oil, natural gas, coal, fish, uranium, or any other natural resource included in an area. These resources are the building blocks of most of the goods manufactured for human use. Even a synthetic (man-made) material such as plastic begins with some natural resource.

Labor

Labor is the contribution of human workers to the production process. While one tends to think of hard, physical work when one hears the term "labor," economists use this term more broadly as well. For an economist, labor includes mental efforts as well as physical ones. It includes both highly skilled and unskilled labor. Open-heart surgery, assembly-line work, janitorial services, and the writing of this book all fall under the category of labor.

Capital refers to all the structures and equipment involved in the manufacturing process. Imagine a factory like the one seen in the photo to the right. The building, the machinery, the tools, the lighting, and the assembly line are all capital. Capital includes the nail guns used by roofers, rags used by employees at a car wash, and the computer used to enter data.

Warehouse

Entrepreneurship is the last factor of production. It is a specific form of labor. It consists of the creative, managerial, and risk-taking capabilities that are involved in starting up and running a business. Entrepreneurship involves organizing the business, developing a business model (i.e. a plan for the conduct of business operations), and raising the funds needed to open for business. Famous entrepreneurs include Bill Gates of Microsoft™, Sam Walton of Wal-Mart/Sam's Club™, and Ray Kroc of McDonald's™.

Sam Walton

Bill Gates

SCARCITY

Every child who grabs a toy in the store only to hear Mom say, "Put that back, we can't afford it," has experienced the frustration of *scarcity*. **Scarcity** is the lack of adequate resources to obtain all of one's wants. Sometimes people confuse the terms "*scarce*" and "*rare*". Hurricanes are *rare* (only a few of them each year), but they are not *scarce* because people do not want even those few. No one produces hurricanes, and even if they could, it's not likely they would sell very well — at least not on the coast. Gold, by comparison,

Gold Bars

is *scarce*. Although there is an abundant supply, there is still not nearly as much gold as people want. Because of this scarcity, people are willing to pay large sums of money for gold. This is how pricing works. The more scarce an item is, the more it costs. An item's scarcity increases and the item becomes more costly, either by becoming rare (there is less of it to go around) or because people want more of it than is available. Conversely, an item's scarcity decreases and it becomes less costly as it becomes more common and/or demand for it diminishes.

STRATEGIES FOR DEALING WITH SCARCITY

Scarcity exists because people's wants are almost always greater than their resources. After Hurricane Katrina in 2005, gas prices in the United States hit record highs. While some accused big oil companies of trying to "gouge" consumers by charging too much, in reality, the problem was actually one of scarcity. Katrina damaged or destroyed a number of oil rigs and refineries. As a result, US oil companies produced less oil than usual and supplies were low. Because gas supplies were *scarce*, producers had less to sell even though consumers (people looking to buy what they want) still

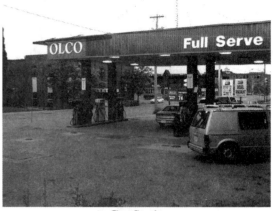
Gas Station

wanted the same amount of gas. In order to still make money and not run out of gasoline, oil companies raised prices to cover the loss in supply. **Higher prices** are one strategy for dealing with scarcity. By raising prices, companies limit the number of consumers who can actually buy the product. They also make sure people don't buy it as often. This allows the producer to still make money while making sure that the limited supply of a product lasts longer than it normally would have.

Shopping

Government regulation is another means for dealing with scarcity. For example, the government might establish a **price ceiling** or a **price floor**, meaning that the price of a certain good or service is not allowed to rise above or drop below a certain level. At times, the government has turned to **rationing**. In other words, it only allows citizens to purchase so much of a scarce good to make sure there is enough to go around. During World War II, for instance, the US government rationed certain products at home in order to make sure there was enough available to supply soldiers with what they needed overseas.

Practice 1.1 Resources and Wants

1. The study of how individuals, firms (businesses), and nations can best allocate their limited resources is called

   A. economics.   C. scarcity calculation.
   B. entrepreneurship.   D. government regulation.

2. When wants exceed resources it is known as
   A. economics.   C. scarcity.
   B. entrepreneurship.   D. productive resources.

3. Describe some strategies used by businesses and governments to deal with scarcity.

1.2 Economic Decision Making

Football Game

The result of scarcity is that economic actors (households, business firms, and governments) must often make choices between two or more options that offer less than what they would like. Consider this dilemma. Tom takes a date to the varsity football game. He decides to go to the concessions stand at half-time. He asks his date, Melissa, what she would like, and then hurries to beat the rush. Melissa wants a soda and nachos. Tom, being really hungry, would like a hot dog, nachos, and a soda. He sees the price list. Hot Dogs....$1.50; Nachos...$2.00; Chips...$0.75; Soda...$1.00. Looking in his wallet, Tom realizes he has only $5.00. Tom is facing the classic economic problem. Because of limited resources (in this case, money), he is forced to make a decision that requires him to choose between options that are all less than ideal. The reality of limited resources requires consumers to follow, either consciously or unconsciously, an economic *decision-making model* that consists of several steps. Using the example of Tom, we can see this model at work.

Decision-making Model

First, Tom must *define the problem.* Doing a quick calculation, he can see that what he wants costs $7.50, and he only has $5.00. Either he or his date will not get what he or she wants.

Hot dog and Coke

Second, he must *list the alternatives.* He could choose Option #1: get what he would like for himself — the hot dog, nachos, and soda, which cost only $4.50. However, this leaves him with only $0.50 left over. He wouldn't even be able to get Melissa a bag of chips. He also would probably not get another date with Melissa (or any girl Melissa knows for that matter). He could choose Option #2: get Melissa's nachos and soda for $3.00, and have $2.00 left over. If so, he can get a hot dog and a drink from the water fountain. He can also choose Option #3: get both of them a hot dog and a soda, and cope with Melissa's disappointment about the nachos. Of course there are other possibilities as well, such as borrowing money from a friend, but time is limited and Tom must choose from these three options.

Third, he must *state the criteria.* What are his priorities? Is filling his stomach most important to him? Is pleasing Melissa? Is not feeling like a selfish person? Tom realizes he doesn't want to be selfish more than he wants to eat. He also realizes that he really likes Melissa and wants another date with her. He decides that his criteria will be to please Melissa.

Fourth, he must *evaluate the alternatives*. In each option (1, 2, and 3), there is a *trade-off*. A **trade-off** is the act of giving up one thing of value to gain another thing of value. Tom values making a good impression on his date, having a full stomach, and feeling good about himself, but each scenario involves a trade-off. He has to give up one thing in order to get another. An **opportunity cost** is the value of the alternative option that is lost when an individual, business, or government makes a decision. In Tom's case, if he chooses to fill himself, his trade-off is the food he could have gotten Melissa; his opportunity cost is a future date with Melissa. On the other hand, if he chooses to buy Melissa her nachos and soda, then his trade-off is the food he could have bought for himself; and his opportunity cost is a full stomach. If he chooses the middle road, then his trade-off is some of the food he could have bought Melissa and part of what he could have gotten for himself; while his opportunity cost is feeling totally full and totally pleasing Melissa.

Finally, Tom must ***make a rational decision***. People, businesses, and governments make rational decisions when they determine that the marginal benefit of an action is equal to or exceeds the marginal costs. **Marginal benefit** refers to the amount of benefit a person, business, or government receives once the cost of their decision is considered. Conversely, **marginal cost** is the cost of the decision once it is weighed against the benefits. If the benefits are greater than the cost, then it is a rational economic decision. However, if the costs exceed any potential benefits, then it is an unwise and irrational decision. Tom decides that the benefit of Melissa's gratitude outweighs the cost of giving up a soda. He chooses Option #2 and gets a drink from the water fountain. Based on his assessment of marginal costs and benefits, for Tom, Option #2 was the most rational choice.

All economic decisions involve trade-offs, opportunity costs, marginal benefits, and marginal costs, regardless if they are made by individuals, businesses, or government.

PRODUCTION POSSIBILITIES

TRADE-OFFS AND PRODUCTION POSSIBILITIES

Since every economic decision involves a trade-off, nations, businesses, and individuals must determine which trade-offs are most beneficial and which ones would be an unwise economic decision. Remember, a **trade-off** involves giving up one option for another. Trade-offs are unavoidable because resources are limited (consumers cannot buy and businesses cannot produce all that they would like because of limit money, modes of production, laborers, etc.). People must decide what goods or services to do without and which ones to spend their scarce resources on. Businesses must decide when it is worthwhile to produce a good or service and when it would not be profitable.

Below is a Production Possibilities Curve. Such a curve depicts how much of a particular product can be produced given the limited amount of resources at a company or individual's disposal (money, capital, laborers, etc.) In the scenario below, Super-J Athletic Company produces football helmets and shoulder pads. Point V represents a point at which Super-J produces more helmets than shoulder pads. Point W represents a point at which it produces more shoulder pads than helmets. Point X represents a point at which it produces an equal amount of helmets and pads. Meanwhile, Point Y is located inside the Production Possibilities Curve and represents a level of production that is inefficient. In other words, more pads, helmets, or both could be produced if resources were maximized (more machines used, laborers put to work, etc.). Finally, Point Z represents a level of production that is not possible because it is outside the realm of the Production Possibilities Curve and cannot be reached with the resources Super-J has available.

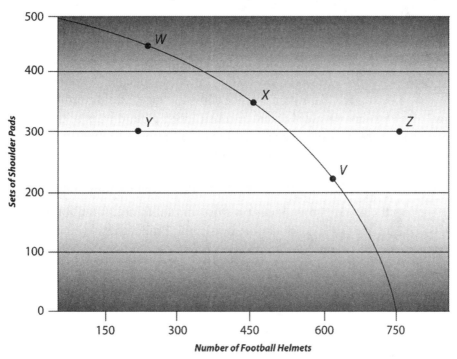

SPECIALIZATION AND VOLUNTARY EXCHANGE

SPECIALIZATION AND DIVISION OF LABOR

Producers want to make as much money as they can selling the goods and/or services they produce. The money that producers make after they have paid for all of their costs are called **profits**. For instance, say you started a business over your summer break mowing lawns. It cost you $10/week for gasoline to fill the lawn mower. You also have to pay your cousin $25/week to borrow his van so you can haul your lawn mower around. Therefore, $35 is your *cost of production*. You then mow five lawns per week at $25 per lawn. Since 25 X 5 = 125, your revenue (money your business takes in) equals $125. However, as we have already mentioned, you had to use $35 to pay for gas and the van. Therefore, while your revenue equals $125 per week, your costs of production equal $35 per week. Since 125-35 = 90, your weekly profit is $90.

Economic Production

In order to maximize profits, producers try to reduce their costs of production. At the same time, they also want to sell their goods/services at as high a price as consumers are willing to pay. Producers reduce their costs by increasing **productivity** (the ability to turn input into output in a certain amount of time). How is productivity increased? One way is through *specialization of labor*. **Specialization** is the devotion of resources (i.e, labor) to a specific task. Instead of one worker trying to do many things, he/she focuses on one particular job. Efficient production of goods and services occurs when specialization is combined with a *division of labor*. **Division of labor** is the act of splitting up work into smaller and more specialized tasks. As a result, more gets produced and with better quality. For example: Let's say you own a shoe factory. At first, each worker is responsible for making pairs of shoes. Each worker must stitch the shoes together, attach the soles, lace the strings, apply the company logo, etc. Unfortunately, the work is very slow. Why? Because each worker is good at constructing certain parts of the shoe, but inefficient at constructing other parts. Some stitch quickly but have trouble attaching soles. Others are great at attaching soles but take a long time to properly apply the company logo. As a result, overall production is slow. However, if each worker specializes and the labor is divided, production increases. Some workers only stitch. Others only apply the soles. Still others lace the shoes and apply logos. Now the workers only focus on those tasks they are suited for. In addition, by focusing, they become even faster and more proficient. Productivity increases and so does profit. This is just one example of how specialization and division of labor work together to increase production.

THE BENEFITS OF VOLUNTARY EXCHANGE

The United States economy is based on **voluntary exchange**. In other words, individuals and businesses freely choose to exchange goods, services, resources, etc. for something else of value (usually money). For the most part, the government does not tell consumers what to buy nor producers what to produce. Both consumers and producers decide for themselves; they make *voluntary decisions*. Of course, there are exceptions. For example, consumers are not allowed to buy illegal drugs, nor are producers allowed to supply things which are illegal or commit fraud (lying about their product to trick people into buying it). Because consumers have the economic freedom to buy what they want (so long as it is legal) and producers the freedom to pursue a profit, entrepreneurs and laborers are motivated to produce goods and/or services that consumers/employers demand. Consumers want to buy goods at as low a cost as possible. Meanwhile, producers hope to sell the goods they produce so as to make as much profit as they can. A voluntary exchange occurs when a consumer finds what they want at a price they are willing to pay and for which the producer is willing to give them the product.

Voluntary exchange has several **benefits**. For one, it encourages increased *productivity and efficiency*. Since producers stand to make more profit if they produce more output, they are motivated to increase their productivity. To do this, they are forever seeking more efficient means of production. This, in turn, encourages technological **inventions and innovations**. Inventions are new products (i.e., machines) that

William Levitt

Levittown

perform a task or fulfill a need that no previous product could perform/fulfill, or at least could not perform nearly as well. The invention of computers is a good example. The first computers were invented during the mid-twentieth century and filled entire rooms. Today, computers can fit on your lap, in the palm of your hand, even in your pocket. Because they allow information to be transferred and processed in mere seconds, computers have totally changed the face of business and communications and have united the world as never before. By comparison, an innovation is any invention or change in process that greatly improves something that already exists (i.e., a faster way to package potato chips). One example of innovation came about in the late 1940s when a developer named William Levitt revolutionized home building. Taking advantage of a demand in the market, Levitt introduced a way to build homes that was much faster and more affordable. As a result, he made a fortune selling homes to middle class citizens who formerly could not afford a house. Levitt's approach forever changed the way developers and consumers approached the housing market. His methods were *innovative* and made him lots of profit by allowing him to increase productivity (i.e., make more homes in less time). Of course, invention often leads to innovation. Take our example of the computer. The invention of the computer led to a faster way to do calculations and process information; however, innovations in computer technology have enabled people to carry and use computers more easily and in more places.

Practice 1.2 Economic Decision Making

1. The act of giving up one thing of value to gain another thing of value is called a/an
   A. opportunity cost.
   B. profit.
   C. marginal cost.
   D. trade-off.

2. Bill wants to buy a shirt for $45 and a hat for $20. However, he only has $50. If he buys the shirt, then his opportunity cost will be
   A. the cost of the shirt.
   B. he cost of the hat.
   C. the enjoyment he would have gotten from the hat.
   D. how comfortable he will feel in the shirt.

3. Define the *marginal cost* and *marginal benefit* and describe the role they play in making a rational economic decision.

1.3 ECONOMIC SYSTEMS

There are four basic types of economic system: *traditional*, *command*, *market*, and *mixed*. Each must answer three fundamental economic questions.

- What will be produced?
- How will it be produced?
- For whom will it be produced?

In addition, who owns the means of production, what motivates producers, and government's role in the market also influence and define economies.

TRADITIONAL ECONOMIES

Traditional Economy

Traditional economies have existed throughout history. Generally, what is produced is whatever has been produced in the past. Laborers in traditional economies usually produce at a subsistence level, making just what they need to survive. A small wealthy class that hands down property and wealth from one generation to the next often owns or controls the factors of production. Because both their occupation and their social status are inherited from their parents, laborers have little opportunity for economic advancement. The upper classes benefit from this system because it protects their wealth and position. Productivity is motivated by both the need to survive and a sense of purpose. Since one's lot in life is predetermined, it is not one's duty to advance to a higher social status, but rather to become an expert in one's assigned role. For example, if you are a ditch digger by birth, then you should strive to be the best ditch digger around.

Traditional economies are not as common today because they usually grow unstable once citizens become aware of other kinds of economic systems. Lower economic classes tend to be drawn either to the opportunities of market systems or the equity of command systems. Meanwhile, the middle and upper classes tend to desire the opportunities for even greater wealth and success present in a market system.

Mowing Grass

COMMAND ECONOMIES

Marx Advocted Communism

In **command economies**, the government owns most of the property and means of production. Private ownership of property is minimal. Government plays the dominant role in that it alone determines what is produced, how much things costs, and how goods and services will be distributed. Distribution is based on **equity**. In other words, output is meant to be distributed equally among the citizenry (at least in theory). Although laborers tend to remain employed, they may or may not have a say in what kind of job they hold and/or under what conditions they work. Since the government owns the businesses, there is little, if any **profit motive** driving production. The incentives to produce are expected to be a sense of duty to the country and/or personal pride. Historically, command economies have proven to be less efficient than market economies. Although they initially attract poorer individuals because of their emphasis on economic equality, in reality, command economies have been susceptible to corruption and greed just as much as market economies. In addition, while national loyalty and personal pride are noble principles, they consistently fail to provide as much motivation for productivity as the promise of financial profit and personal advancement. Therefore, since economic conditions are set by the government rather than consumer demand and market competition, there is very little innovation in a command economy because potential innovators don't have the incentive of financial gain.

Finally, command economies, because they are centralized, tend to be slow to react to changes in demand. As a result, they often produce too much of something that is not desired and too little of something for which there is a market. For example, in the former Soviet Union, it was not uncommon to see people lined up around the block waiting to buy scarce products like a loaf of bread or a roll of toilet paper. In short, command economies seriously limit voluntary exchange. Producers must produce what they are told, and consumers are limited in what they can buy and from whom they can buy it.

Adam Smith, Early Advocate of Free-Markets

MARKET ECONOMIES

Business Owner

In a **market economy**, producers and consumers determine what gets made and for whom. Property and factors of production (land, labor, capital, and entrepreneurship) are privately owned, with the government owning only enough to carry out its limited and defined role. Producers decide what to produce based on what consumers demand and what prices consumers are willing to pay. The motivating factor for producers is profit and for laborers, higher wages/salaries and/or personal advancement. Since producers compete with one another in the market, consumers tend to have many of choices and can shop around for what they want at the lowest possible price. Innovation thrives as producers constantly seek new ways to outdo competitors. The government interferes very little in a market economy, preferring to let supply and demand steer the market.

Strengths And Weaknesses Of Different Economic Systems:

Type of Economy	Strengths	Weaknesses
Command	The strengths of a command economy are that they provide *greater security* than market economies because job opportunities are often dictated by the government and employment protected by the state. In addition, income tends to be distributed equally (at least in theory) with no one having too much or too little.	Because there is no profit motive for producers and very little chance of advancement for workers, command economies tend to operate inefficiently because there is no incentive to be innovative or to improve production. Command economies greatly restrict freedom by limiting what consumers may buy, what producers may produce, and what careers people may pursue. Without innovations and the incentives for economic gain provided by private ownership, command economies tend to develop slowly, experience limited growth, and lag behind market economies.
Market	Market economies provide a great amount of freedom for producers, consumers, and workers. Because businesses tend to be privately owned by people trying to maximize profits, innovations and specialization usually make market economies far more efficient and likely to experience growth and prosperity than command economies.	The weaknesses of market economies are that they offer less security and can often produce inequality when it comes to wealth. Although people in a market economy enjoy the freedom to start a business or pursue the career of their choice, they also run a greater risk of failure. Since the government does not regulate or control the economy, it does not guarantee citizens a job or an income. In addition, since some citizens are more successful than others, market economies tend to offer less economic equity. Society tends to become divided between a relatively small upper class that possesses most of the wealth, a large middle class that possesses a modest amount of wealth, and a lower class that possesses very little wealth.

MIXED ECONOMIES

New York

Just about every economic system is, in reality, a **mixed economy**. In other words, they have elements of more than one system that make up their economic framework. The US is a mixed economy in that it offers great freedom to economic actors (producers and consumers) while at the same time implementing enough government control to hopefully avoid economic catastrophes (i.e., depression, massive inflation, crucial shortages of needed goods, etc.). Although it is based on free-market principles, the United States is not a pure market system.

Hong Kong

By contrast, China (also a mixed economy) falls closer to a command economy. The state owns much of the means of production and exercises tight control over the nation's economy. Still, in order to compete internationally and keep their economy moving, China allows a certain amount of private ownership and market competition.

THE ROLE OF GOVERNMENT IN A MARKET-ECONOMY

Why would the government choose to take an active role in a market economy (making it, in reality, a mixed economy)? For one, profit motive does not naturally provide everything that consumers need. It takes the government to provide certain **public goods and services**. For instance, national defense, police and fire protection, public parks, etc. are all services provided by the government. The government provides them because society needs such services regardless of how profitable they might, or might not, be. In addition, in order to maintain

Police Officers

stability in society and preserve public order, governments often choose to **redistribute income**. In other words, they take money from citizens who have it (usually through taxes) and give it to citizens who don't (normally through welfare programs). Often, when societies have experienced turmoil or governments have been toppled by their own citizens, it has been because of an angry class of poor citizens. By redistributing income, governments can help meet the needs of poorer citizens and hopefully maintain stability. Of course, such measures often anger and frustrate richer citizens who feel that they have worked hard for their money and should be free to spend it as they wish without being forced to give it to support government programs.

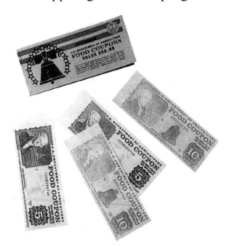

Welfare

Ben Bernake

The government will also intervene to **resolve market failures**. In order to avoid an economic crisis, the government will, from time to time, jump in and interfere with the natural economic cycle. For example, in the 1930s, the US experienced its worst financial crisis in history: the Great Depression. President Franklin D. Roosevelt responded with what he called the "New Deal." It was a series of government policies and programs aimed at regulating the economy in hopes of restoring prosperity. Although it did not end the depression, it did provide some relief and is an example of how government regulations can be used to deal with market failures. Today, **common ways the government tries to regulate the economy** include tariffs (taxes on foreign imports to give US manufacturers an advantage), subsidies (money paid to make up for losses in an industry), actions by the Federal Reserve (the nation's central bank), environmental regulations, workplace safety guidelines, and consumer protection laws.

The Great Depression

Franklin D. Roosevelt

Finally, the government also passes laws and enforces regulations to protect **property rights**. The ability to own one's own property is a key element in a market economy. The chance to own one's own business, labor, house, etc. is what provides much of the incentive that drives the economy. Therefore, the government usually tries to protect property rights because it knows that, by doing so, it is indirectly stimulating the economy as well.

DEREGULATION

Government also makes an impact when it chooses to **deregulate** (stop or decrease its regulation) an industry. One example of this occurred in the 1970s when President Jimmy Carter deregulated the airline industry. Before Carter took such action, the airline industry benefited from a system which practically guaranteed it a profit. It was the government that set fares, determined routes, and finalized schedules. As a result of this setup, however, consumers found themselves paying higher prices and often dissatisfied with service. By deregulating the airlines, Carter suddenly threw the airline industry into the realm of free-market competition. This had great economic impact as suddenly airlines found themselves having to produce more efficiently and compete to survive. Railroads, trucking, telecommunications, and energy production are all industries which have experienced various degrees of government deregulation. When the government deregulates, it tends to increase competition and, ultimately, product quality. However, if not careful, a lack of regulation can also leave the door open for less safety in the workplace, manufacturing techniques that damage the environment, unfair labor policies, and/or civil rights abuses. For this reason, the government must walk a fine line between maintaining an efficient market economy and protecting social welfare.

Airline

Jimmy Carter

Practice 1.3 Economic Systems

1. A command economy is an economic system in which

    A.   the government owns much of the property.

    B.   individual property rights are very important.

    C.   consumer demand determines what will be produced.

    D.   profit motive is the main motivation for producers.

2. Which of the following is a strength of a market economy?

    A.   guaranteed equity.

    B.   guaranteed employment.

    C.   opportunity for profit.

    D.   lots of government regulation to ensure that no one has too little or too much.

3. What are some of the ways the government might try to regulate the economy in a mixed-market economy, and why might the government want to take such measures?

1.4 INVESTMENT

PRODUCTIVITY

As mentioned earlier, **productivity** is the rate at which goods and services are produced. The more goods and services that can be produced in a set amount of time, the greater the productivity. Productivity is a key factor in determining economic growth. Increased productivity means that there are more goods available to buyers and — assuming a competitive labor market — financial rewards for laborers (i.e., larger incomes and career advancement).

Assembly Line

When considering productivity, one must look at both *inputs* and *outputs*. **Inputs** are all the factors of production that go into producing a good or service. Inputs include machinery, labor, goods a producer must purchase in order to make their product, etc. **Output** is simply the amount of good or service produced. In order for a producer to be productive, they must make enough of a good or service to earn a profit. In order to earn a profit, the inputs they purchase must create enough output to earn income greater than their cost of production. Take for example, a company that makes clothes. To make a profit, the company might produce and sell enough shirts to earn more money than what it had to spend on all of the cotton, buttons, etc. to make the shirts in the first place.

THE IMPACT OF INVESTMENT

NYSE

How can a business or worker increase productivity? Through *investments*. **Investment** is using resources that could bring immediate benefits for the purpose of gaining greater benefits at a later time. One example is financial investment, such as people buying stocks or putting money in 401k plans at work. People who invest financially loan their money to banks or other businesses rather than spending it. They then collect the money later after it has accumulated interest. **Interest** is money paid to an investor in exchange for the use of their money.

Production often grows due to **capital investment**. This is investment in capital goods and human capital. **Capital goods** are those products used to make other goods or provide services. For example, bolts and metal used to produce car engines, plastic and wiring used to manufacture computers, and a van used by a courier service to deliver packages are all examples of capital goods. Investing in capital goods can increase productivity by allowing a worker to do more work in a given time frame. Capital goods should be distinguished from

Capital Investment

consumer goods, which are those items purchased for final use by individuals, households, and/or firms. A pair of skis, a toaster, or a bottle of your favorite soft drink, are all examples of consumer goods.

Meanwhile, **human capital** refers to investment in people. For instance, when a company pays for its employees' health insurance, time off to spend with a new baby, tuition to go back to school, or additional professional training, it is investing in human capital. By investing money, time, and resources to improve their employees' quality of life and skills, they hope to improve their business as well.

Laborers also invest to increase productivity. They do this by spending time, energy, and money on education and training. Through education and training, people increase their knowledge, skills, and value as workers (employers are willing to pay more for labor that is highly educated and well-trained). For example, by choosing to spend time and energy (and money if you bought it yourself) reading this book, you are making an *investment* that will hopefully make you better educated and more productive. This will, in turn, make you more valuable to potential employers when you go to look for a job. It is important to remember, however, that not all education and training requires a classroom or a book — it can take place on the job or through real-world experiences. In general, the more educated workers are, the more their skills and services are in demand. As a result, businesses are willing to pay more money to get them. This means that educated employees tend to enjoy a **higher standard of living** than less educated workers. In other words, they make more money and can afford more things than less

Job Training

Employees

educated workers. In addition to education/training, taking care of one's physical condition is also an investment in human capital. Through exercise, eating right, getting enough rest, etc., workers tend to be more alert and productive.

For both producers and laborers, there are always trade-offs and opportunity costs to investments. Choosing to buy new machinery means less immediate returns on production. Spending time studying for a test means giving up doing something more enjoyable or relaxing. Investments are made when the long-term return is considered more valuable than the pleasure that would be received from using the same time or money for immediate gratification.

Practice 1.4 Investment

1. The rate at which goods and services can be produced is called
    A. capital investment.   C. producer price output.
    B. productivity.   D. human capital.

2. If a factory owner uses some of her profits to purchase new machinery, she is investing in
    A. human capital.   C. output returns.
    B. the Producer Price Index.   D. capital goods.

3. Define *investment* and give some examples.

4. Define *output* and *input*. What role does each play in productivity?

CHAPTER 1 REVIEW

Key terms and concepts

economics	benefits of voluntary exchange
wants	inventions
resources	innovation
land	traditional economies
labor	command economies
capital	market economy
entrepreneurship	mixed economy
scarcity	public goods and services
higher prices	redistribution of income
government regulation	resolve market failures
supply and demand	common ways the government tries to regulate the economy
price ceiling	property rights
price floor	deregulation
rationing	productivity
trade-off	input
opportunity cost	output
rational decisions	investment
marginal benefit	interest
marginal cost	capital investment
profit	capital goods
specialization	human capital
division of labor	higher standard of living
voluntary exchange	

Multiple Choice Questions:

1. Trees, minerals, and the real estate on which a company builds its main manufacturing center are all

   A. capital goods.   C. land.

   B. capital investments.   D. entrepreneurship.

2. Following a massive hurricane that hits Georgia's northern coast, residents have no running water or electricity. As a result, citizens buy up all of the flashlights and bottled water in the area faster than producers can resupply them. What problem do people on the Georgia coast now face regarding flashlights and bottled water?

   A. excessive regulation   C. rationing

   B. scarcity   D. incomplete trade-offs

3. Which of the following tends to make economies more efficient?

   A. specialization

   B. government ownership of property

   C. income redistribution

   D. regulations aimed at economic equity

4. Martha owns her own company. She invests in all the capital goods needed to make her product and sells her goods with the motivation of making huge profits. So long as she does not produce anything illegal, Martha freely chooses what to produce and consumers freely choose whether or not to buy her product. It sounds like Martha's company operates in a

   A. command economy.   C. traditional economy.

   B. market economy.   D. economy based on equity.

5. The greater the profit motive in an economic system, the greater the likelihood of

   A. innovation.

   B. equity.

   C. security.

   D. government controlling the factors of production.

6. Higher prices and government regulation are both strategies for

   A. increasing consumption.   C. dealing with scarcity.

   B. encouraging economic equity.   D. aiding entrepreneurship.

7. Jamie must make an economic decision. He must choose whether or not to buy a new truck. After considering all the options, he concludes that the marginal costs of the truck are greater than the marginal benefits. In Jamie's case, buying the truck would be
   - A. a rational economic decision.
   - B. an irrational economic decision.
   - C. an opportunity cost.
   - D. a productive choice.

8. Common ways the government might try to regulate a mixed-market economy include
   - A. deregulation.
   - B. forbidding any private ownership of property.
   - C. imposing tariffs or subsidies.
   - D. lifting environmental restriction

9. Buying stocks, purchasing new equipment for a business, paying for employees training, and purchasing the latest computers for one's office are all examples of
   - A. opportunity costs.
   - B. economic outputs.
   - C. productivity.
   - D. investment.

10. Which of the following is an example of investing in human capital?
   - A. buying a new company truck
   - B. an employee asking for a raise
   - C. paying for an employee's health insurance
   - D. requiring employees to document what they are doing at work

Chapter 2
Microeconomic Concepts

SSEMI1	The student will explain why limited productive resources and unlimited wants result in scarcity, opportunity costs, and trade-offs for individuals, businesses, and governments.
SSEMI2	The student will give examples of how rational decision making entails comparing the marginal benefits and the marginal costs of an action.
SSEMI3	The student will explain how specialization and voluntary exchange between buyers and sellers increase the satisfaction of both parties.
SSEMI4	The student will compare and contrast different economic systems and explain how they answer the three basic economic questions of what to produce, how to produce, and for whom to produce.

2.1 ECONOMIC INTERDEPENDENCE AND THE FLOW OF MONEY

THE CIRCULAR FLOW OF ECONOMIC ACTIVITY

There are three fundamental actors when it comes to economic activity: *households*, *businesses*, and *government*. A **household** is an individual or group of individuals that occupy a single housing unit (apartment, condo, or house) and shares common living expenses. A household might be a blood-related family. However, it might also consist of people who live together and share expenses but are not blood-related. A **business**, on the other hand, is an individual or group that works to produce a certain good or service. In a market economy, businesses (also called firms) produce for the purpose of a profit. Finally, the **government** provides law and order, structure, and even necessary goods and services that might otherwise not be provided by what the market demands (i.e., national defense, maintaining public parks and monuments, etc.). **Microeconomics** is the study of how these economic actors make decisions and are impacted by the allocation of resources.

Individuals who make up households supply labor to businesses in exchange for money. These businesses then use this labor to produce goods which households and other businesses buy and consume. Both households and businesses pay taxes to the government. The government uses their tax dollars to provide things that are meant to benefit society. In addition, the government also uses revenue to purchase goods from private businesses and pay wages/salaries to households in exchange for the labor of government workers. As you can see, households, businesses, and government depend on each other in order for the economy to function smoothly. This mutual need is referred to as

Family Dinner

economic interdependence. Households provide labor and act as consumers. Businesses act as producers *and* consumers (i.e., they need to purchase things necessary to run their business), and government acts as both a producer and a consumer as it provides structure and some regulation. The economic flow of money between households, businesses, and government is called the **circular flow of economic activity**. This "flow" is depicted in the diagram below.

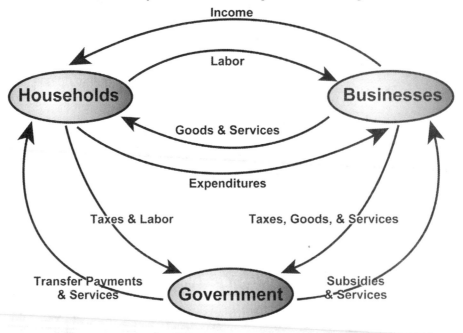

PRODUCT AND RESOURCE MARKETS

Product Market

Goods that are sold to consumers for final consumption are sold in the **product market**. Running shoes sold to a jogger, pencils sold to a student, frozen dinners sold to a busy mom, etc. are all examples of goods sold in a product market. The product market is where producers seek to earn their profits. However, producers also purchase goods for the purpose of improving and/or increasing production. Such goods are said to be sold in the **resource**, **or factors**, **market** because they involve the four factors of production (land, capital, labor, and entrepreneurship). The resource/factor market is where producers invest in new capital to increase production. It is also where employers find the labor necessary to run their businesses.

Resource Market

THE ROLE OF MONEY

Most of us take the existence of money for granted. We fail to realize that its invention was one of the greatest innovations in world history. Prior to its existence, most early civilizations relied on a *barter system*. People had to trade goods that they possessed for goods that they

Money

Economic Exchange

wanted. As you might imagine, it wasn't always easy to find the person with the good or service you wanted who was willing to exchange it for the good or service you had to offer. Money became a **medium of exchange** that solved this problem because it could be assessed a value and then exchanged for any number of goods in a market place. Without money as a form of economic exchange, it would be very difficult for economic activity to function efficiently outside of small communities.

Most people use the term "money" interchangeably with *currency* . Currency refers to both coins (metal currency, such as pennies, dimes, etc.) and notes (paper money). Economists, however, use the term "money" much more broadly. Anything that acts as both a medium of exchange and a standard of value is considered money. Nearly everyone exchanges and invests money on a daily basis. Individuals, businesses, and even the government must make decisions about how to invest and spend money. Today, money is still often exchanged physically, such as when you hand a salesperson a $50 bill in exchange for a new shirt. However, with advances in computer technology and the internet, money is often exchanged electronically through bank transactions, online stock trades, debit card transactions, and online bill payments as well.

Online Transaction

Practice 2.1 Economic Interdependence and the Flow of Money

1. The three major actors in terms of economic activity are

   A. governments, businesses, and producers.

   B. households, individuals, and the stock market.

   C. households, businesses, and government.

   D. leaders, people, and firms.

2. Heathcorp depends on Bill's computer skills to keep their company adequately serving its customers so that Heathcorp can continue to earn annual profits. In exchange, Heathcorp pays Bill a salary that he depends on to pay his bills. Bill and Heathcorp both pay taxes to help support the government which provides them with protection. This scenario is an example of

   A. economic interdependence.   C. capital investment.

   B. government regulation.'   D. investment in human capital.

3. Describe the important role played by money as a medium of economic exchange.

2.2 ECONOMIC INFLUENCES

LAW OF SUPPLY AND DEMAND

In a market economy, buyers and sellers determine what will be produced and for whom. This occurs through what is commonly referred to as the **law of supply and demand**. *Supply* refers to how much of a certain good is available to consumers. *Demand* refers to how much consumers want the particular good. The *law of supply* states that producers will only produce a good that will yield them profit because it is something that consumers want. This means that, in order for there to be any supply of a certain good, producers must be convinced that producing the good will make them money. They have no incentive to produce a product that will cost them more to produce than the amount for which they can sell it. Likewise, they also have no incentive to produce more of a certain product than people are willing to buy at the price producers are willing to sell. In other words, producers will stop producing a good once their marginal cost begins to equal or exceed their marginal benefit. By comparison, the *law of demand* states that consumers will only demand/buy a product for which they have a need or want and that is set at a price they are willing and

Supply

Demand

able to pay. The more they desire a product and the more scarce that good is, the more they will be willing to pay to get it. However, the more available a product is (i.e., it is available from several competing producers) or the less they desire the good, the less they are willing to pay. Thus, the *law of supply and demand* states that supply (what is produced) will be determined by what is demanded (what consumers will buy). If there is sufficient demand for a good, then producers will supply it so long as they can make a profit. On the other hand, if there is no demand, or if demand is not great enough to earn a profit, producers will not supply it. If the profit that a company can receive is considered high, many producers will enter the market to produce that good or service. However, if the profit they receive is relatively low, only a small number of producers (i.e. those who can make the product for the lowest cost and highest profit) will enter the market.

Producers will also cut back on production once supply begins to exceed demand. For instance, say a company invents an electrical heater that allows you to heat your whole house without ever turning on the gas, thereby saving you hundreds of dollars in heating bills. The product might sell like hot cakes in December and January, but come April, demand will fall off drastically. The *law of supply and demand* suggests that the producer of this product will produce much larger amounts of the product during the winter months when there is high demand than during the summer months when demand is small. During the winter, the potential profit is far greater than the marginal cost of producing each heater. However, as the weather grows warm, the heaters don't sell fast enough to justify making them at the same pace. Therefore, production will drop to the level of demand.

INFLUENCES ON SUPPLY AND DEMAND

PRICE

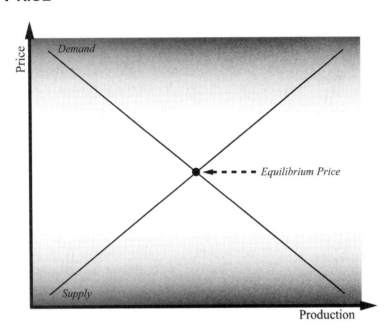

Equilibrium Price

Several factors influence supply and demand. One important factor is **price** (the amount of money for which producers are willing to sell their products to consumers). There may be demand for a good, but if producers don't believe they can earn a sufficient profit, it will either not be produced, or will only be produced by those firms that can mass produce enough to make the profit they require. The price at which producers are willing to make the same amount of a product that consumers demand, is called the **equilibrium**, or **market clearing**, **price**. In theory, the market clearing price will result in every unit produced being sold. Why? The reason is that supply is perfectly equal to demand. It may be easier to understand this concept if one considers it graphically. The graph to the right shows a supply curve and a demand curve. The **supply curve** (or supply schedule) tells us how much of the product that sellers are willing to part with at various price levels. The **demand curve** (or demand schedule) tells us how much of the product buyers are willing to purchase at various prices levels. The point at which the two curves meet is the equilibrium price. Any price below the equilibrium price will result in less supply because producers are not making enough to continue producing the product. Conversely, any price above the equilibrium price will result in lessening demand because fewer consumers are willing to pay for it. In a free market economy, prices are set as supply and demand naturally steer the market towards the equilibrium price. Since, in reality, markets very rarely hit equilibrium for any length of time, it is accurate to think of free-market economies as constantly moving towards equilibrium, with certain price levels coming closer to the target than others.

SHORTAGES & SURPLUSES

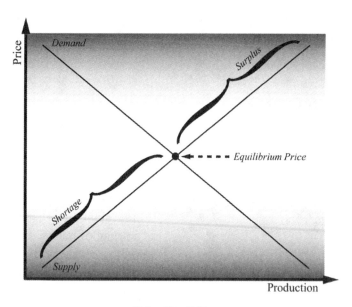

Price Elasticity

When supply of a certain good falls short of demand, the market is said to have a **shortage**. Conversely, when supply exceeds demand, the market has a **surplus**. The graph to the right shows not only the equilibrium price, but also the results of prices above or below the equilibrium price. A price above equilibrium results in a surplus. A price below equilibrium results in a shortage. If prices are too high, people will not buy the product. Therefore, producers will not be able to sell all that they have. On the other hand, if prices are too low, people will buy up all that is available faster than producers can produce more. Thus, many people who demand the product will be left without. When there is a shortage, prices increase because the product in demand is more scarce and people are willing to pay more to get the small amount that is available. When there is a surplus, prices fall because there is more than demanded and those consumers that do want the product have a lot of options regarding where to get it. Therefore, producers must compete (i.e., lower prices) to convince these consumers to buy from them. Otherwise, producers will be stuck with goods/services that they paid to produce but from which they make no profit. As you can see, the amount of a good supplied by producers and the amount demanded by consumers greatly affects price. Conversely, price greatly affects how much suppliers are willing to produce and the degree of demand as well. The sensitivity of price to supply and demand and its tendency to fluctuate as supply and demand change is referred to as **price elasticity**. In other words, price is not set. It changes depending on supply and demand. The more a change in price affects supply and/or demand, the greater a products price elasticity. For example, if the cost of hot dogs is raised from $2 to $6, demand for hot dogs will change drastically because many of the people who would buy a hot dog at $2 will not pay $6 for one. However, if the cost of having a dentist treat an infected tooth jumps from $500 to $650, demand will likely not drop off because people who are in pain with an infected tooth still want the treatment. Although they may grumble about the price increase, it does not affect their demand for the service. In this comparison, hot dogs have a high price elasticity, whereas dental care does not.

As you can see, the quantity (amount) available of a good is one factor that impacts price. It is important to note that there is a difference between change in *quantity demanded* and change in *demand*. Change in quantity demanded simply means that the amount demanded has changed, although the amount people want may not have. This can occur because of changes in supply without any change in overall demand (i.e. people may want the same amount of the good, they just buy more or less because the supply is larger or smaller). Sound confusing? Maybe this example will help illustrate what we're talking about. Imagine that a hail storm moves through

Florida and severely damages the orange crop. The damaged crop does not cause people to want less orange juice, but consumers will end up buying less and at a higher price because there is less orange juice available. By contrast, a *change in demand* is a change in the amount of product that consumers actually want. For instance, residents in Savannah, Georgia, might not demand much plywood most of the time. However, when a hurricane is headed toward the coast, the demand for plywood increases drastically. People want more of this product at any price than they did previously.

There is also a difference between *quantity supplied* and *supply*. A *change in the quantity supplied* is a change in the amount producers sell that may or may not be linked to a change in the overall willingness to supply products at different price levels. Take, for instance, oil companies in the US. Since just about every adult in the US drives a car, there is an overwhelming demand for their product. However, suppose a war breaks out in the Middle East (which often happens) and imports of oil fall. Although demand alone would dictate a high level of supply, other circumstances intervene to cause the quantity supplied to be less than market forces alone would have dictated. By comparison, *a change in supply* is a change in the amounts that producers are willing to sell at all prices. Say ten years from now, a company begins to mass market a car that runs on water instead of gas. Now, the number of businesses producing oil drops, but for totally different reasons. This time, it is because demand has dropped and the market dictates that there is not enough profit to continue production.

CONSUMER TASTES

Designer Jeans

Supply and demand is also affected by **consumers' tastes**. What is desirable to one consumer may not be desirable to another. Consider the following example of how consumer taste can impact price. Teresa is 17 years old and wants to get a new pair of blue jeans. She sees the pair she wants at a well-known, upscale fashion store for $125. Since she forgot to bring her credit card, Teresa decides she will come back the next day and buy them. That evening, she runs to Discount Kingdom to buy some hair spray and notices in the clothes section that they have a cheaper brand of jeans that look exactly like the pair she wants for only $35. The decision seems simple. Forget the $125 pair and buy the lower priced jeans. However, what if Teresa's top priority is not price? What if she can afford either pair and her top priority is the status symbol of wearing jeans from the upscale store? If so, Teresa will choose the $125 pair of jeans rather than the $35 jeans. While some might argue Teresa is too shallow and not very practical, this is a perfect example of how consumer tastes impacts supply and demand. The upscale store can afford to set prices above what they normally would in the market because they know that enough consumers want the status of their label, prefer the way their jeans fit, have been convinced by advertising that anything less than their jeans won't do, and so on. How much a consumer values status, what a consumer considers comfortable or attractive, and what producers a consumer trusts are all ways in which a consumer's individual taste can help set price and impact supply and demand.

SUBSTITUTE AND COMPLIMENTARY GOODS

Supply and demand will also be affected by *complimentary* and *substitute goods*. **Substitute goods** are goods that can be used in place of other goods. For example, both hot dogs and tacos are foods that can be bought at the convenience store for lunch. If one buys a hot dog, then they are less likely to buy a taco (unless they are really hungry and/or enjoy heartburn). The more substitute goods there are for a particular product, the more competition producers face in trying to convince consumers to buy their particular good. **Complimentary goods**, on the other hand, are goods that work together to fulfill a certain need. For instance, DVDs and DVD players are both useless

DVD and Player

unless used together. Therefore, the more the demand for DVDs goes up, the more the demand for DVD players increases as well. Whereas consumers purchase substitute goods *instead* of buying another product, they purchase complimentary goods *because* they have another product.

INFLATION AND INTEREST RATES

A general rise in prices for most products throughout an economy is called **inflation**. When you ask for $20 to go to the movies and get a lecture from your parents about how, when they were kids, movies cost $2 and a box of popcorn 75 cents, you are listening to (or, at least pretending to listen to) your parents rant about inflation. As the costs of production increase, firms are willing to produce less at given prices. Therefore, to cover their costs and still make a profit, they raise prices. However, inflation should also lead to increased employment and wages because businesses are increasing profits. Therefore people have more money to spend. In a perfectly even inflation, prices will end up higher but production will remain exactly the same. The opposite is true of **deflation,** which is a general fall in prices. An even deflation should lead to lower prices but the same amount of production. In reality, there are many factors that can affect inflation and deflation, preventing them from occurring "evenly." Because inflation features a rise in prices, it directly affects supply and demand. As inflation rises, people tend to save their money rather than spend it on high-priced products. This leads to less demand, which leads to less supply, and eventually should bring prices back down so that consumers can once again afford to spend money in the economy.

Bank

Interest rates are another economic factor. An **interest rate** is the amount of money a borrower pays to a lender in exchange for the use of that lender's money. Credit card companies, banks, lenders who offer school loans, and the credit union that financed your car all charge interest rates. Consumers, however, also earn interest when they open bank accounts. For instance, if you put $100 into an account that paid 2% interest annually, at the end of one year, you would have $100 X 0.02 = $102. When interest rates are higher, consumers are more likely to save rather than spend. They want to earn interest on the money they've saved rather than pay high interest rates on credit cards or large purchases (like homes or cars). On the other hand, if interest rates are low, consumers are more willing to spend. Therefore, when interest rates are high, demand is lower and prices tend to fall to encourage consumers to spend money they are inclined to save. Conversely, when interest rates are low, demand and prices tend to rise as consumers are inclined to spend.

GOVERNMENT ACTION: WAGE AND PRICE CONTROLS

Filling up Car

As mentioned before, the US government regulates and manipulates the economy to some degree. It sometimes does this through **wage and price controls**. For example, the government sets a **minimum wage**. This is the minimum amount that producers can pay employees for their labor.

Minimum Wage Worker

Those who support a minimum wage argue that anything less would not provide an adequate standard of living. While the intent of this wage control might be good, in reality, it also creates a surplus of labor that leaves many unemployed. This is because businesses only have so much money to spend on labor. For example, say Pedro owns a business. He wants to hire Mike, Frank, and Kevin. However, if he hires all three, he cannot afford to pay them all the minimum wage required by the government. Therefore, Pedro hires Mike and Frank at the minimum wage and leaves Kevin unemployed. Had Pedro been free to pay them what he wanted, he could have also hired Kevin. The government has also been known to set **price floors** (minimum price below which the price of a good or service is not permitted to drop) and **price ceilings** (maximum price above which the price of a good is not permitted to rise). For instance, the government might set a price floor on agricultural products to protect US farmers from bankruptcy, or a price ceiling on rents to ensure lower income families can afford a home. While such solutions as price ceilings and price floors may sound appealing, it is important to remember that they do not adhere to normal laws governing the marketplace and, therefore, have economic costs as well as benefits. Setting price floors can lead to inefficient production and surpluses as producers continue to produce goods for which there is no demand. Meanwhile, Price ceilings can often produce shortages. Since Hurricane Katrina in 2005, many US citizens have demanded that the government set a ceiling on gas prices. Oil companies and some government leaders have been quick to point out, however, that if an artificial ceiling is imposed on gas prices during a time in which oil supplies are short, then consumers will have less incentive to conserve fuel and change their driving habits. As a result, people will continue to buy gas much like they always have, eventually causing the supply of gas to run out.

Practice 2.2 Economic Influence

1. The principle that producers will only produce goods that will yield them a profit because it is something consumers want is known as the

   A. law of supply.   C. equilibrium price.
   B. law of demand.   D. price elasticity.

2. The principle that consumers will only buy products which they need or want and which are priced at a cost they can afford is known as the

   A. law of supply.   C. consumer taste.
   B. law of demand.   D. wage and price controls.

3. One side-effect of price ceilings is that they produce

   A. equilibrium.   B. surpluses.   C. shortages.   D. inflation.

2.3 COMPETITION

Another economic factor is **competition**. How many producers are supplying a particular good? The more suppliers there are, the more options for consumers. The more options for consumers there are, the more producers must compete for business. In order to compete, producers must either lower prices as much as they can while still making sufficient profit, or quit producing the particular good. Take, for instance, Wally's small coffee shop on the corner. It is a local business with only one location. Unfortunately for Wally, he has to close his business

Business at Work

because a huge coffee-house chain has opened down the street. Why must he close? Because the chain is so big and sells so many cups of coffee, it can offer customers lower prices, special deals, etc. Wally cannot afford to compete because he can't make up in volume what he would lose in profit if he charged the same low price. Because consumers want to pay as low a price as possible and because they have a choice, they stop going to Wally's and go to the big chain. Thus, Wally closes and the supply of coffee in the neighborhood decreases. Now the big chain is the only producer of a good cup of coffee. In turn, it can now raise prices because, while demand for coffee is the same, there is now only one supplier. Since there are now fewer options for consumers (only one coffee shop instead of two) people are willing to pay the big chain more than they would have when they could have gone to Wally's.

FREE-MARKET COMPETITION

Walmart vs. Target

A market system is one in which buyers (consumers) and sellers (producers) come together to exchange things of value (i.e., money for goods). A market that features **pure competition** is one in which businesses can compete with each other fairly, without any government regulations or non-economic factors dictating price, supply, or demand for a product. In a purely competitive market, producers can enter the market easily with no individual buyer or seller buying or selling enough to change the price of a particular good or service. For a perfectly competitive market to occur, four factors must be present:

- There must be a large number of buyers and sellers.

- Products must have the same quality.

- There must be no major barriers to entering market.

- There must be a free exchange of price information. That is, consumers and producers must have access to what each producer is charging for their goods.

In many cases, these conditions more or less exist. Consider, for instance, the wheat market. There are so many wheat farmers that no single one of them can raise or lower the market price of wheat by how much they individually supply. At the same time, so many different companies around the world are bidding for wheat that none of them can lower the price by withholding their bid. The wheat market is relatively competitive.

Monopolistic competition is somewhat different from pure competition. In pure competition, the competing products are basically the same. One company's gasoline, oil, grain, etc. can easily be exchanged for another's without the consumer noticing much difference in quality. Price is the determining factor in who consumers buy from and how much products will be in demand. However, in monopolistic competition, products are similar but not identical in quality. Examples of monopolistically competitive markets include the market for soft-drinks, fast food

Clothing Store

burgers, restaurants, coffee shops, automobiles, computer games, clothes, etc. If someone strongly prefers Coke to Pepsi or wants to drive a BMW instead of a Toyota Corolla, then they will likely be willing to pay more for the product they want even though the cheaper item could potentially serve the same purpose. Although there may be a large number of producers who enjoy easy access to the market (just like in pure competition), price alone is not the only determining factor affecting what people buy or how much they're willing to pay. Product quality and consumer taste are also important. As a result, since consumers cannot replace the good as easily as they could in a pure-competition market, producers can influence the market price by how much they produce and choose to charge for their specific good.

Auto Competitors   **Coke vs. Pepsi**

Fast Food Competition

EFFECTS OF FREE-MARKET COMPETITION

Price Checking

Free-market competition keeps prices down. When several producers supply the same or similar goods, they must compete for consumers. Since consumers want to spend as little as possible to get the goods they want, producers must keep prices low enough to compete for their business. In addition, free-market competition also encourages invention and innovation. Since businesses are always trying to outdo their competitors, they are constantly looking for new ways to improve their products, make them more appealing to consumers, and improve production. The invention of the light bulb, television, advances in computer technology, more efficient assembly lines in factories, and breakthroughs in medical technology are all examples of inventions or innovations that came about as entrepreneurs attempted to compete for consumers in hopes of making a profit. Finally, competition also improves quality and customer service. Since the market has multiple producers, businesses know that the quality of what they sell must be as good as, if not better than, what their competitors supply. After all, if you produce cars that break down every 10,000 miles and your competitor's cars only break down every 50,000 miles, you are going to eventually get clobbered in the marketplace. Demand for your competitor's product will increase while demand for your product falls. For consumers, then, free-market competition is generally a good thing.

MONOPOLIES AND OLIGOPOLIES

Georgia Power

While no one company can corner (control) the market on an entire industry under perfect competition, there are situations where perfect competition does not exist. A **monopoly** is a market structure in which there is only one producer of a given good or service, and in which there are no adequate substitutes. For example, if only one company supplied electricity or made cars, these would be examples of monopolies. For a monopoly to exist, there must be barriers that prevent other firms from entering the market. Since a monopoly is the only supplier of a good or service that is in demand, it is able to dictate the industry price of that good or service by how much it produces. In general, monopolies charge higher prices, produce less output, and provide less quality than a competitive market. This is because they have no competition. If consumers aren't totally satisfied, the monopoly doesn't have to worry or improve. After all, the consumer has nowhere else to go for the good. In command economies, it is the government that often exercises a monopoly (review chapter 1, section 1.3).

Another market structure that prevents perfect competition is the *oligopoly*. An **oligopoly** is a market in which there are only a few producers. Typically, oligopolies form in industries which must necessarily be large (i.e., companies that provide utilities like electrical power or natural gas). Oligopolies operate in a manner between competitive markets and monopolies. Unlike perfect competition, the oligopolist firms can affect the price of a product. However, unlike a monopoly, the oligopoly must observe and take into account the actions of its competitors. Oligopolists must be responsive to price changes because they will lose market share quickly if they are not. It is also relatively easy for the members of an oligopoly to conspire to control prices just as a monopoly would. For this reason, there are laws to prevent such actions.

Practice 2.3 Competition

1. Competition in the market place has which of the following effects?

    A. It promotes innovation.

    B. It encourages surpluses.

    C. It leads to inefficient production.

    D. It protects businesses from financial risk.

2. What are monopolies and oligopolies? How do they tend to differ from businesses in a market where there is free-market competition? Why do they exhibit such differences?

3. Describe the differences and similarities between monopolistic competition and pure competition.

2.4 THE ORGANIZATION AND ROLE OF BUSINESS

TYPES OF BUSINESSES

Businesses play an important role in the US economy. Businesses produce goods and services that consumers desperately need (such as food, clothes, medical care, etc.) and/or want (ipods, motorcycles, athletic shoes, televisions, etc.) Businesses are also often the source of innovation and invention. They invent things and come up with more efficient ways of doing things in their effort to produce more and increase their profits.

SOLE PROPRIETORSHIP

Thousands of US businesses operate every year. These businesses are organized in a number of different ways. The simplest form of business is the *sole proprietorship*. A **sole proprietorship** is a business owned by an individual or the members of a household. Remember Wally's coffee shop? That was a sole proprietorship because it was owned only by Wally. The advantages of a sole proprietorship are flexibility, personal charm, direct interaction between owners and consumers, and the fact that business decisions can be made quickly by one

Sole Proprietorship

owner. However, proprietorships have disadvantages as well. First, the proprietor has *unlimited liability*. In other words, he/she is responsible for all debts incurred by the business. Proprietorships also have a *limited life*, which means that they cease to function at the same time that their owners do. For the company to continue after the original owner's death or retirement, it must be reorganized under new ownership. Third, proprietors usually have limited funds available to them and have to obtain startup money by taking out loans from banks or other financial institutions.

PARTNERSHIP

Some businesses are organized as *partnerships*. A **partnership** is a type of business in which two or more people pool their resources and share the risks and profits of the business. Law firms, doctors offices, and accounting firms are often partnerships. The advantages of a partnership are that they can raise more money than sole proprietorships and combine expertise. However, there are disadvantages as well. First, unlike a sole proprietorship, it may be difficult to reach decisions that satisfy all the partners. A second disadvantage is the legal complication of dissolving the partnership if it should break up. Proprietorships simply perish if the owner quits or dies, but a partnership must decide whether to remain in business and, if not, who gets what. The third major disadvantage of the partnership is that the partners are completely responsible for the debts incurred by the business. Although several individuals share the debt, because partnerships are often larger, their debts are usually greater as well.

CORPORATION

Corporation

New York Stock Exchange

The third type of business is a *corporation*. A **corporation** is a firm that exists as a legal entity in the same way a person does, and which is usually owned by a number of shareholders (although much smaller businesses and even individuals can incorporate, as well). Shareholders buy **stock** in the corporation, thereby granting them a share of ownership proportional to how much stock they own. Many corporations sell their stock on a stock market (a market where anyone can buy or sell stocks in available companies). Stock markets are important institutions in a market economy because they are primary vehicles for investment. The rise or fall of major stock markets (i.e., the New York Stock Exchange) is a major indicator of how the economy is doing overall. A major advantage of the corporation is that it offers *limited liability*. Individual shareholders can only lose what they invest in the corporation and are not liable for all the debts that the corporation incurs. In other words, if you buy $1000 worth of stock in a corporation that has $1,000,000 in debt and the corporation goes under, you only lose $1000; you aren't stuck with the whole million. **Bonds** are another way that some companies raise money. Whereas buying stocks makes the purchaser part owner in a company, bonds are a means of *loaning* money. A person loans a certain amount of money to either the government or a private entity in exchange for the bond. They then collect interest on the loan in addition to cashing in the bond (getting their money back) at a later time. There are other advantages to corporations, as well. Selling shares means they can raise large amounts of money in a short period of time. Without the corporation, people would not be willing to invest in gigantic firms because of the huge personal risk such investments entail. Corporations also have *unlimited life*. They live on past the death of individuals. Corporations also have disadvantages, however. One is double taxation. The corporation, as a legal entity, is taxed based on the profits it earns. Shareholders are often then taxed again on any *dividends* (payments made to shareholders from the profits of the firm) and/or capital gains (money earned by selling an asset--i.e., some of their stock--at a higher price than one purchased it). Corporations may also suffer from internal conflict. The shareholders (owners) and the hired management may not agree on how to proceed with the business. Shareholders may prefer that profits be paid as dividends, while managers may want to reinvest profits in capital goods. Over time, shareholders can also lose control of the corporation as other stockholders acquire larger shares and gain more influence.

FRANCHISE

McDonalds Franchise

Finally, there are **franchises**. These are businesses in which sole proprietors or partnerships purchase the local rights to a trademark corporation. For instance, McDonalds™ is a massive multi-national corporation; but the local McDonalds

Fast Food Eating

where you grab a Big Mac and fries is probably franchised to an individual owner or partnership. The franchise owner must pay a licensing fee and maintain contractual agreements with the trademark corporation. The benefits of a franchise are the name recognition and backup support that national chains can provide. The disadvantage is the lack of flexibility and limited creativity that owners have. Because they represent a national chain, they must do things a certain way and sell only certain products.

Practice 2.4 The Organization and Role of Business

1. Bernice owns her own local gift shop. She acquired the necessary loans to open it, assumes all the financial risks herself, and makes all the decisions. It sounds like Bernice's business is a/an

    A. franchise.   C. corporation.

    B. partnership.   D. sole proprietorship.

2. Bill lives in Macon, Georgia. However, he just bought fifty shares of stock in a large business headquartered in Chicago, Illinois. Bill's stock gives him a small piece of ownership in the business at limited financial risk. It sounds like Bill has invested in a

    A. sole proprietorship.   C. partnership.

    B. corporation.   D. franchise.

3. Compare and contrast the similarities and differences between sole proprietorships, corporations, and partnerships. Include the advantages and disadvantages of each.

CHAPTER 2 REVIEW

Key terms and concepts

household	substitute goods
business	complimentry goods
government	inflation
microeconomics	deflation
economic interdependence	interest rate
circular flow of economic activity	minimum wage
product market	wage and price controls
resource, or factors market	price floor
medium of exchange	price ceilings
law of supply and demand	competition
law of supply	price competition
law of demand	monopoly
demand	oligopoly
supply	sole proprietorship
price	partnership
equilibrium, or market-clearing, price	corporation
shortage	stock
surplus	bonds
price elasticity	franchises
consumers' tastes	

Multiple Choice Questions

1. Jordan works for the state of Georgia as a probation officer. His labor provides the government with a much needed service. In return, the state pays Jordan a salary. With his salary, Jordan purchases the goods he needs/wants from private firms. He also pays taxes that allow the government to continue to provide protection and government services. Jordan's economic interdependence with the government and private businesses is referred to as what?

    A. the money flow   C. circular flow of economic activity

    B. the monetary cycle   D. economic independence

"If the public wants this football team to remain in this city, then they will buy season tickets. If they do not, then the tickets will not sell. However, this organization will not continue to lose money on this team. If this city does not appreciate what they have, then we are prepared to move to another city where the fans are waiting in expectation for us to come, and they are anxious to pay to see the product we put on the field."

2. The above quote is an indirect reference to which of the following?
   A. a factors market
   B. law of supply and demand
   C. disagreement over equilibrium price
   D. the security encouraged by a free-market system

3. Byron has just received an annual bonus at work for $2000. Currently, interest rates are very high. The year before, Byron received a bonus check for $1200 when interest rates were very low. Which of the following statements is MOST LIKELY true?
   A. Byron spent his bonus last year and will spend it again this year.
   B. Byron saved his bonus last year and will save this year's check, too.
   C. Byron spent his bonus last year, but this year will save it.
   D. Byron saved his bonus last year, but this year will spend it.

4. Money can BEST be defined as which of the following?
   A. currency
   B. a medium of exchange
   C. something that transfers risk from one party to another
   D. interest

5. Frank has owned the same Italian bistro in the heart of the city for nearly 23 years. Although it's small, it's known for the best lasagna in town. What kind of business does Frank operate?
   A. sole proprietorship   B. partnership   C. cooperative   D. corporation

6. Barry and two associates have been operating a business that is not going well. Barry is stressed out because the company is over $200,000 in debt and he knows that if it goes under, he and his two associates will have to pay it out of their own pockets. It sounds like Barry and his two associates have a
   A. sole proprietorship.   B. partnership.   C. stock.   D. corporation.

7. A market structure in which only one producer supplies a good that is in demand, thereby permitting them to set the price by how much they supply, is called a
   A. competition.   C. oligopoly.
   B. monopoly.   D. conglomerate.

8. A business that manufactures ice-skates buys steel for their blades in a

   A. products market.   C. demand curve.

   B. resource market.   D. elastic price variation.

9. Look at the diagram below and answer the following question:

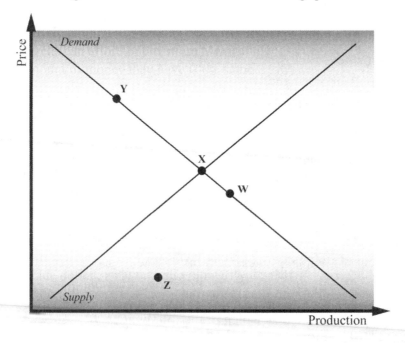

What point represents the equilibrium price?

   A. W   B. X   C. Y   D. Z

10. Albert is the CEO of a company that provides sugar to much of the United States. Unfortunately, a huge hurricane swept through the Gulf Coast and wiped out much of this year's sugarcane crop. Albert's company will likely take what action?

   A. close their business.

   B. raise sugar prices.

   C. lower sugar prices.

   D. ask the government to impose a price ceiling.

11. The following year, Albert's company benefits from an abundant sugarcane crop. However, due to recent scientific evidence that declares sugar to be bad for peoples' health, there is not nearly as much demand for sugar as there is supply. Which of the following actions will lead sugar farmers to continue to grow sugar despite the lack of demand?

   A. a government imposed price floor on sugar.

   B. a government imposed price ceiling on sugar.

   C. free-market competition.

   D. the law of supply and demand.

Chapter 3
Macroeconomic Concepts

SSEMA1	The student will explain why limited productive resources and unlimited wants result in scarcity, opportunity costs, and trade-offs for individuals, businesses, and governments.
SSEMA2	The student will give examples of how rational decision making entails comparing the marginal benefits and the marginal costs of an action.
SSEMA3	The student will explain how specialization and voluntary exchange between buyers and sellers increase the satisfaction of both parties.

3.1 Measuring Economic Activity

In this chapter, we will study *macroeconomics*. **Macroeconomics** is the study of the economics of a nation as a whole. Macroeconomics examines the effects of events on the economy in *aggregate* (in total). When studying macroeconomics, it is important to understand how nations and economists measure and evaluate economic activity.

GDP, CPI, and the National Debt

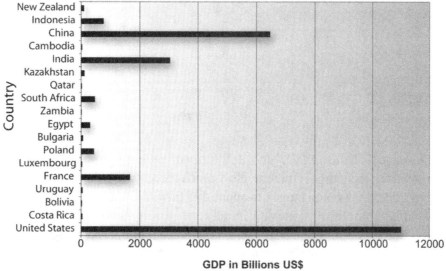

Economists use several *economic indicators* to monitor how well the national economy is doing. Economic indicators provide facts, data, etc., that help show the present and/or future health of the economy. One means is by calculating the nation's **gross domestic product (GDP)**. The GDP is the total value of all final goods and services produced in an economy. The more final goods and services an economy produces, the healthier it is generally considered. Some economists also like to look at *per capita GDP*, which measures the amount of goods and services produced per household. By measuring GDP per household, economists believe they can better determine the standard of living in a particular society. Another economic indicator is the **consumer price index (CPI)**. The CPI measures monthly changes in the costs of goods and services by monitoring the prices of goods/services that are typically purchased by consumers. A rise in prices is called **inflation**. Inflation often occurs when consumer demand is high and/or supply is short. As a result, producers charge more for their products. Inflation usually leads to a rise in employment as higher prices bring in more profits for producers and allow them to expand production and hire more workers. Conversely, a fall in prices is called **deflation**. Deflation often leads to greater unemployment because producers don't earn as much profit and often have to lay-off workers or refrain from hiring new employees in order to stay in business. On rare occasions, inflation and rising unemployment rates can occur at the same time. This creates a double economic nightmare as goods cost more and people are out of work. When prices and unemployment rise simultaneously it is called **stagflation**.

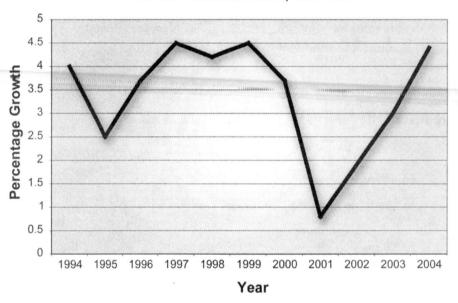

Economists also look at the *national debt* and *national deficit*. The **national debt** is the amount of money owed by the federal government. How much money the government owes affects its decisions regarding how much money to spend and how much money to collect in taxes. This, in turn, greatly affects how much money businesses and citizens have, thereby affecting the economy. By comparison, the **national deficit** refers to how much money over budget the government is in a given year. For instance, if the government has a budget of $10 billion for 2007 and ends up spending $11 billion, then the government has a deficit of $1 billion. Whenever the government finishes the year at a deficit, the national debt increases because the government owes even more money. However, whenever the government spends less money than it budgeted for the year (known as a *national surplus*) the national debt can decrease as the government chooses to use that money to pay off some of what it owes.

TRADE AND EMPLOYMENT

When GDP grows, the CPI remains at a level that increases profits without indicating rampant inflation, and the national debt shrinks (or, at least, remains stable), the nation is usually said to be experiencing **economic growth**. In other words, the economy is expanding and doing well. Other factors determine economic growth as well.

NET EXPORTS

Nations export and import goods and resources for producing goods on a constant basis. *Exports* are goods or resources a nation sells to other countries, thereby bringing foreign money into the economy. *Imports* are goods and resources a nation buys from other countries, thereby sending money out of the national economy. A country's **net exports** are the amount of goods or resources a nation is exporting and selling once one subtracts the amount of total imports from total exports.

Chinese Workers

TOTAL NUMBER OF EXPORTS - TOTAL NUMBER OF IMPORTS = NET EXPORTS

Japanese Export

For example, let's say that the United States is exporting 100,000 units of good A to Japan, while Japan is exporting 200,000 units of good B to the US. Assuming that neither country is trading any other goods with any other countries, Japan would have a net export of 100,000 units (200,000 Japanese exports - 100,000 imports from the US), and the United States would have a net export of -100,000 units (100,000 US exports - 200,000 imports from Japan). In reality, of course, all nations have multiple countries they trade with while exporting and importing multiple goods. Hopefully, however, this simple example helps you understand the concept of net exports.

Why are net exports important when it comes to macroeconomics? The more a nation exports, the more money tends to flow *into* the economy. That means more money for businesses; higher wages for employees; more money to spend on capital goods; increased production; greater profits; more jobs; and more options for consumers. It also means more money for the government because people have money to pay taxes. On the other hand, the more a nation imports, the more money goes *out* of the economy. As money goes out, US businesses make less, often have to decrease production, and people often lose their jobs as companies cannot afford to hire or do not need them. The government also cannot tax companies and individuals as easily without causing drastic economic affects because their is less money. For this reason, positive net exports are generally considered to be signs of a growing economy.

Interestingly, although the US is generally viewed as the healthiest economy in the world, the United States has consistently experienced a *trade deficit* since the 1970s. It tends to import more than it exports. However, although countries may import more than they export, that *doesn't necessarily mean they aren't experiencing profitable trade.* For instance, a nation may import a large amount of raw materials very cheaply, then use them to manufacture finished goods that they then export at greatly increased prices. (We will discuss trade and its effects on the US more in chapter 4.)

Trade

UNEMPLOYMENT

Another factor that affects the national economy is the unemployment rate. Anyone who is able and wants to work, yet does not have a job, is considered to be "unemployed." The unemployment rate is the percentage of the total labor force that is not working. The labor force is the number of people over the age of 16 who would like to work. It is important to recognize that unemployment rates do not reflect those people who are not part of the workforce either because they are physically or mentally incapable of work or because they voluntarily choose not to work (e.g. some college students and stay-at-home parents).

Seeking Employment

Unemployment

There are several types of unemployment. **Cyclical unemployment** is caused by a lack of adequate demand for products. During times of economic hardship when consumers have less to spend and demand for products drop, businesses make less profit. As a result, they produce less and need fewer employees. This means that they don't hire people they ordinarily would have and may even let some of the employees they already have go. The result is higher unemployment. It is called *cyclical* because, as the economy improves and consumers have more money to spend, demand, production and the need for workers will increase, lowering the rate of unemployment.

Structural unemployment, on the other hand, is caused by changes in the nature of production. For example, in recent years, more and more grocery stores and mega-store chains have begun using automatic check-out systems. These are computerized systems that allow customers to check-out using a debit or credit card, without needing the assistance of a clerk. Stores like using them because it allows them to still check-out customers without having to pay an extra employee. As a result, they need fewer employees, have to pay less in wages, and, therefore, have more profit that can be used on capital investments, etc. Of course, the unfortunate side-effect for those who work as store clerks is that, as such computerized systems become more popular, more and more of them will lose their jobs.

Structural Unemployment

Unemployment will increase because the *structure* has changed. This change in structure means that the services these workers supply are no longer in demand the way they used to be. Therefore, fewer of them have jobs. Unlike cyclical unemployment, their positions have nothing to do with how the economy is doing. In fact, it might be that the technology that is taking their place is doing so during a time of economic growth. Their jobs won't be coming back with a change in the economic cycle. They will have to find other kinds of work; a process that will take time and, in many cases, additional training. Fortunately, such unemployment does not occur overnight. It usually is the result of a process that takes place over time. After all, when you go to the grocery store, you still see lots of clerks working in addition to the self check-out stations. This is because many customers are used to and still want personalized help. It will take time before computers totally take over such jobs. Hopefully, the period in-between when new technology is introduced and when certain jobs become totally obsolete will be long and gradual enough to allow most employees time to acquire the new skills they need to find other jobs. Because the nature of the economy is always changing, there is always some degree of structural unemployment.

Working

Frictional unemployment is another type of unemployment. It is the period individuals experience between the time they leave one job and the time they take another. Frictional unemployment may be caused by structural factors, cyclical factors, being fired for incompetence, or could be the result of voluntarily leaving a job one doesn't like in order to find a job one likes better.

Shopping Mall

Seasonal Employment

Finally, **seasonal unemployment** results from changes in the output of various industries throughout the year. A beach resort at Jekyll Island may hire a lot of people during the summer when business is booming, then let them go during the winter months. Conversely, ski resorts in the North Carolina mountains are likely to hire more

employees in the winter while laying them off spring through fall. Home builders tend to hire more employees in the warm months when the weather permits lots of construction, then cut back on their number of employees when the weather turns cold and wet. Retail stores often hire more salespeople for the holidays, only to turn some loose after the heavy shopping season passes. These are just a few examples of seasonal unemployment. The good thing about seasonal unemployment is that workers tend to know ahead of time when they can expect to work and when they better have another job lined up. As as result, seasonal unemployment often doesn't catch laid-off workers by surprise and cause the kind of unexpected financial stress that cyclical, frictional, and structural unemployment often do.

THE EFFECTS OF SPENDING DECISIONS

HOUSEHOLD AND BUSINESS SPENDING

Paycheck

As mentioned before, there are three primary economic actors: households, businesses, and government. How these actors choose to spend money has a great impact on the economy. When households spend money, it is called **consumer spending**. The total amount of consumer spending is called **consumption**. The more consumers spend in the economy, the more the economy tends to expand and grow. Why? When consumers spend, businesses increase their profits. This leads to more production, more jobs, etc. Consumption leads to increased **business spending** because businesses have more money to spend on capital investments, production processes, and hiring new employees. On the other hand, when consumers spend less, businesses often have to reduce prices, make less profits, and unemployment tends to rise. Less consumption usually leads to less business spending because companies are making less money. In general, then, high consumption is an important part of maintaining economic growth.

In addition, overall levels of income, employment, and prices play a role in the spending decisions that affect the economy. **Income** is the amount of money taken in by households. Most people think of income in terms of how much money people are paid in exchange for their labor. For instance, if you are hired out of college by a large corporation at a starting salary of $45,000 per year, then $45,000 is your income. The less taxes are taken out of that $45,000, the more income you have left over to spend and/or save. Again, the circular flow of

Suburbs

economic activity between households, businesses, and government is important when we are studying macroeconomics. When governments charge lower taxes, consumers have more to spend. The money consumers have left over after taxes is called **disposable income**. When they spend more money on products produced by businesses, businesses can afford to raise prices and make more profit. In turn, businesses now have more money to hire people and/or raise the income of their employees. As incomes increase, people have even more to spend. This increases businesses profits further, allowing businesses to continue hiring and increasing workers' wages. While various other factors come into play to affect income levels and prices as well, you can hopefully see how income and spending interact to affect the economy.

GOVERNMENT SPENDING

Government spending also affects the economy in several ways. Obviously, the government has to have money before it can spend it. The money the government takes in is called *revenue*. Most revenue is collected through taxes. The federal, national, and local governments all collect taxes in one form or another. For instance, both the federal government and most states collect an *income tax* based on how much money people make each year. They also collect *capital gains tax* based on a percentage of how much money people and businesses make

Tax Return

from annual investments. Businesses are often taxed based on how much profit they made in a given year. States often require citizens to pay taxes on the automobiles they own. Meanwhile, local governments often require people to pay *property taxes* on homes or land they own within a county or municipality. How the government chooses to tax citizens/businesses and spend the revenue it raises is called **fiscal policy**. Governments collect taxes to raise revenue because they need money to pay for national defense, public education, highway construction, police and fire protection, garbage collection, the maintenance of public spaces (parks and monuments), and any welfare programs they may offer. Fiscal policy is determined by the legislative branch of government, however it usually requires the approval of the executive branch as well. In the case of the federal government, Congress has the power to pass tax laws, but the president has the power to either sign or veto them. (If he/she signs them they become law. If he/she vetoes them they don't, unless 2/3 of each house of Congress votes to override the veto.)

Ronald Reagan
Fiscal Conservative

Ted Kennedy
Fiscal Liberal

Newt Gingrich
Fiscal Conservative

Walter Mondale
Fiscal Liberal

Generally, the more governments spend on government programs, national defense, education, welfare, health care programs, etc. the higher it must raise taxes. Otherwise, the government starts to run annual deficits and its debt increases. This means that consumers (households) and businesses have to pay more in taxes and have less to spend on consumption, production, hiring, etc. As a result, consumer spending and business spending tend to decrease. Such a decrease can slow economic growth. Therefore, while the government may have lots of things it would like to spend money on, leaders have to remember that raising taxes tends to discourage spending and can hurt the economy. On the other hand, the more governments decrease spending, the less tax revenue it requires. By lowering taxes, the government leaves more money in consumers' pockets. This encourages spending because people have more money. As households spend, business spending increases as well and encourages economic growth. Once again, however, the government must be careful. While low taxes tend to stimulate the economy, they also produce less revenue. This means that the government has less money to spend on social and economic programs that might help better the lives of certain citizens. **Fiscal conservatives** are people who favor lower taxes and less government spending. They don't want the government funding welfare programs, but would rather see social needs met by private citizens, organizations, and businesses. By contrast, **fiscal liberals** favor a more active government and would rather have higher taxes so that the government can afford to fund social programs. Since both conservatives and liberals are continually elected to political office, how much the government will require its citizens to pay in taxes and how it will spend its revenue are often topics of intense political debate.

It is worth noting that governments also spend money on programs meant to stimulate economic growth. For example, during the 1930s, the United States experienced its worst financial crisis in history: the Great Depression. During the depression, the stock

Wall Street

market crashed, businesses failed, and nearly one-fourth of the nation was unemployed. President Franklin Roosevelt initiated a program called the "New Deal", in which the government spent money on various programs that were designed to put people back to work and encourage spending. Although the New Deal did not end the Depression, it did provide some hope. Today, some point to the New Deal as a historical example of how government spending can help the economy. Others, however, argue that the New Deal actually hurt the economy more than it helped it. They claim that the less government spends on any kind of program, the better. Regardless of who's right, everyone agrees that government spending decisions greatly impact the national economy.

AGGREGATE SUPPLY AND DEMAND

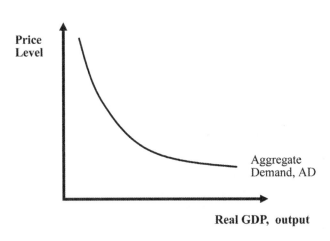

Aggregate supply is the supply of all products in an economy. **Aggregate demand** is the demand for all products combined. The overall price level of goods is determined largely by aggregate supply and demand. If, in general, the supply of goods in an economy is equal to, or nearly equal to, the aggregate demand, then the economy is said to experience equilibrium. (Of course, within the overall supply and demand of goods there will likely be some goods for which demand exceeds supply--a shortage--and some for which supply exceeds demand--a surplus. Overall, however, aggregate supply and demand is balanced.) On the other hand, if aggregate supply exceeds aggregate demand, then the economy experiences an overall surplus, resulting in a drop in prices that could hurt the economy if it occurs too fast. (Such a phenomenon is called "overproduction." Overproduction was one of the major causes of the Great Depression mentioned earlier.) By the same token, an economy could experience a situation in which aggregate demand exceeds aggregate supply. This results in an overall economic shortage. Such a shortage usually leads to inflation as producers raise prices to cover the lack of production and to ensure that supply does not run out. Once again, if the economic change (this time a rise in prices) occurs too drastically, it can cause negative affects on the economy as people can no longer afford to pay high prices and stop consuming certain products. When aggregate supply roughly equals aggregate demand, it is generally considered to be a sign of a healthy and stable economy.

THE BUSINESS CYCLE

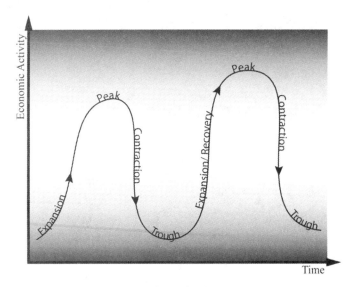

Business Cycle

Roller Coaster

The US economy is similar to a roller coaster. Sometimes it makes its way uphill on a slow, steady rise. Then, just after it reaches the peak, it comes racing back down! Such economic ups and downs are called the **business cycle**. The business cycle has four main parts: *trough, expansion, peak,* and *contraction*. The amount of time each part lasts varies depending on the circumstances. The steady ride up is called **expansion**, because the economy is growing. Many times it leads to a *recovery* because this growth often occurs after a less prosperous period. Expansion/recovery is sparked by something that happens to jump-start the economy. Government spending programs, corporate tax breaks, increased investments, and/or even a war that increases demands for production (i.e., WWII) can lead to recovery. Whatever the reason, the economy improves as companies produce more goods, employment increases, and people are able to buy more. As the "roller coaster" inches its way to the top, the expansion reaches its **peak**. This period is defined by *prosperity*, in which production is high, unemployment low, and wages increase. The peak period only last for a time, however, before the economy starts to come down. This period is known as **contraction** and is characterized by a fall in production, rising interest rates, declining profits, and a slowdown in capital investments. Demand falls as consumers stop buying goods. As businesses sell less, they make less. As a result, they stop hiring and even lay employees off; thereby raising unemployment. If this trend lasts for 6 to 8 months, the economy experiences a **recession**. A recession is a decline in the nation's GDP and/or negative economic growth for a period of more than 6 months. Eventually, the economy hits its low point: its **trough**. The trough period is a time of high unemployment, low economic production, and falling stock prices. If it continues to worsen and last a long time, the nation may even slip into a **depression.** A depression is an extended period in which a nation's economy slows severely, causing hardship for households, businesses, and the government.

Practice 3.1 Measuring Economic Activity

1. The total value of all final goods and services produced in an economy is called the

   A. Gross Domestic Product   C. Business Cycle

   B. Consumer Price Index   D. Net Export

2. When consumption increases, employment usually

   A. remains the same.   C. increases.

   B. decreases.   D. enters stagflation.

3. Higher taxes tend to

   A. increase consumption.   C. cause inflation.

   B. increase unemployment.   D. lessen government spending.

4. What are net exports and why would a nation want positive net exports overall?

5. Describe the difference between cyclical, structural, and frictional unemployment.

6. What is a recession?

3.2 THE FEDERAL RESERVE SYSTEM

Federal Reserve Bank Minneapolis

**Federal Reserve Head Quarters
Washington D.C.**

As discussed in the previous section, the government can affect the economy through **fiscal policy** (how it spends money and imposes taxes). Fiscal policy is set by the executive and legislative branches of government. Normally, the executive branch may propose a spending budget, but it is up to the legislative branch to ultimately approve it. Also, the legislative branch must pass laws raising or reducing taxes. However, the executive branch may veto any tax bill it does not agree with.

Fiscal policy is not the only way the government impacts the economy. The US government also features a central bank that is independent of the influence of any branch of government. This bank is known as the **Federal Reserve**. Its purpose is to strictly control the money supply. In other words, it works to regulate how much money is flowing into the nation's economy during a given period. It does this through what is called **monetary policy**. By controlling the money supply, the Federal Reserve (often called "the Fed") can help control inflation, encourage consumer spending, motivate people to save rather than buy, etc. Since monetary policy allows the Federal Reserve to control the flow of money, it allows the government to exercise a great amount of control over prices in the marketplace. Therefore, the Federal Reserve uses monetary policy to try and encourage economic growth by ensuring that prices and employment stay stable.

ORGANIZATION OF THE FEDERAL RESERVE SYSTEM

Although its chairman and members of its board of governors are appointed by the president of the United States, the Federal Reserve operates independently of all three branches of the federal government. Other than having to deliver an annual report to the House of Representatives, the Fed does not have to take orders from Congress or the president. It is important that the Federal Reserve be independent because the executive and legislative branches of government both have incentives from

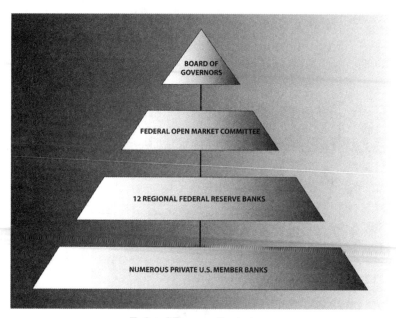

Federal Reserve System

time to time to engage in inflationary spending and the printing of more money. This could have terrible effects on the economy if the Federal Reserve were not free to resist such policies.

Ben Bernanke

The Federal Reserve is headed by a **board of governors**. Board members are appointed by the president and cannot be removed unless it can be proven that they have behaved in an unethical fashion. The board is responsible for setting monetary policy and is headed by a Federal Reserve chairman. Currently, Ben Bernanke is the chairman of the Federal Reserve.

The Federal Reserve also consists of the **Federal Open Market Committee**, which is responsible for overseeing open market operations (see section below on monetary policy: open market operations). In addition, there are several **Federal Reserve Banks**. The Federal Reserve Banks are located in selected major cities throughout the country and act as a financial agent/resource for member banks within their region. Finally, there are the Federal Reserve's **member banks**. Member banks are private banking organizations which are governed by the Federal Reserve. All national banks are required to be member banks of the Fed, while many state-chartered banks ultimately become members as well.

Federal Reserve Banks

1- Boston   7- Chicago
2- New York   8- St. Louis
3- Philadelphia 9- Minneapolis
4- Cleveland   10- Kansas City
5- Richmond   11- Dallas
6- Atlanta   12- San Francisco

Federal Reserve Map

MONETARY POLICY

RESERVE REQUIREMENT

Bank Loan

The Federal Reserve controls the flow of money in several ways. One is through its ability to determine banks' *reserve requirement*. Banks are required to keep a certain amount of money on hand, rather than loaning it to borrowers. The **reserve requirement** is the percentage of a bank's money that must be kept on hand rather than loaned. This percentage is set by the Federal Reserve. When the Fed sets a higher reserve requirement, it decreases the amount of money circulating in the economy because it requires banks to hold on to more of their money, rather than loaning it to households and/or businesses that would then spend it in the economy. Such a policy is called a **"tight money" policy** because it makes money "tighter." On the other hand, if the Fed lowers the reserve requirement, then more money is pumped into the economy because banks are able to loan more to people who then spend it. A low reserve requirement is called an **"easy money" policy** because it is "easier" for money to circulate in the economy.

Buying a Car

Just in case this sounds confusing, let's look at a practical example of how the Federal Reserve can affect the economy through its regulation of the reserve requirement. Say that 100 people want to buy a house. They all go to the bank to take out a loan for the purchase. The Federal Reserve, however, has just instituted a "tight money" policy. This means that the bank has to keep more money on hand and has less money to lend. As a result, the bank does not have the resources to grant all 100 households a loan. It can only loan money to 60 households. What consequences does this have? In addition to disappointing the 40 households that couldn't get a loan, it also means that 40 houses will not be bought that otherwise would have been. This means less money for the developer, fewer construction workers hired, less contractors employed, less demand for house inspectors, and less income for real estate agents. These people, in turn, will now have less income to spend in the marketplace. Store owners will not sell as much, fewer cars will be sold by auto dealers, fewer patrons will eat at restaurants, and so on. On the other hand, if the Federal Reserve institutes an "easy money" policy, then the bank loans more money, more homes are bought, incomes increase, more money is spent, production tends to rise, etc.

DISCOUNT RATE

The second way the Federal Reserve impacts the nation's money supply is through the *discount rate*. The **discount rate** is the interest rate that banks and other financial institutions pay the Fed in order to borrow money. In other words, the Federal Reserve acts like a "bank for banks." Banks and other financial institutions can borrow money from the Fed, and then — just like a household or business that borrows from the bank — pay it back with interest. An *interest rate* is a percentage that a lender charges a borrower in exchange for a loan. The higher the discount rate charged by the Fed, the higher the interest rate banks must charge borrowers in order to still make money. Higher interest rates encourage people to save, rather than borrow and spend, because they would rather *earn* high interest on money that they are saving than have to *pay* high interest on money that they are borrowing. As a result, the money supply decreases as more money sits in savings and less is spent in the economy. Conversely, a lower discount rate allows banks to charge lower interest. This results in more loans and spending, causing the money supply to go up.

OPEN MARKET OPERATIONS

Finally, the Fed uses **open market operations** (the sale or purchase of US treasury bonds) to control the flow of money. These bonds are a means of loaning money to the government. Those who purchase bonds are paid interest in exchange for the government's use of their money. Eventually, they are able to cash in the bond for the amount that they loaned plus any interest earned. When the Fed *sells* securities (bonds), it lowers the money supply and serves to fight inflation. How so? Understand that bonds are a form of saving for investors. They buy the bond to gain interest and then get their money back at a later time. Money that is saved (i.e., invested in bonds) is money that is not spent in the market. Therefore, the more securities sold, the more the money supply decreases as people and businesses buy bonds rather than spend. In addition, when the Fed sells securities, bank reserves of money decrease as households and businesses purchase bonds rather than saving their money in banks. Banks then have to borrow more from the Federal Reserve to keep the reserve requirement on hand. The Fed then must raise the discount rate in order to make sure banks don't borrow too much. This, in turn, raises interest rates and leads to less spending and less money in circulation. (See the previous paragraph regarding the discount rate.) However, when the Fed *buys* securities, it is putting money back into the hands of people and businesses who can then spend it in the marketplace. This causes interest rates to drop, spending increases and more money is pumped into the economy. Can you see now how important the Federal Reserve is?

Practice 3.2   The Federal Reserve System

1. After much debate in Congress, the House and Senate finally pass a bill calling for a 1% tax decrease and a cut in federal funding to artistic institutions. The president then signs the bill. This is an example of the government's

    A.   fiscal policy.
    B.   monetary policy.
    C.   open market operations.
    D.   tight money policy.

2. The central bank of the United States that sets policies designed to control the money supply is called the

    A.   Congressional Bank.
    B.   Bank of the United States of America.
    C.   Federal Reserve.
    D.   Bank of US Governors.

3. What is the *discount rate*? Describe how raising it affects the nation's money supply.

4. What is the difference between a "tight money" policy and an "easy money" policy? How does each affect the nation's money supply?

5. What is meant by the term "open market operations"? Describe how the government uses open market operations to impact the money supply.

CHAPTER 3 REVIEW

Key Terms and Concepts

macroeconomics	fiscal liberals
gross domestic product (GDP)	aggregate demand
consumer price index (CPI)	aggregate supply
inflation	business cycle
deflation	expansion
stagflation	peak
national debt	contraction
national deficit	recession
economic growth	trough
net exports	depression
unemployment rate	The Federal Reserve
cyclical unemployment	monetary policy
structural unemployment	board of governors
frictional unemployment	Federal Open Market Committee
seasonal unemployment	Federal Reserve Bank
consumer spending	member banks
consumption	reserve requirement
income	"tight money" policy
disposal income	"easy money" policy
fiscal policy	open market operation
fiscal conservatives	

Multiple Choice Questions:

1. The ups and downs that the nation's economy goes through is officially referred to as what?

    A. a roller coaster   C.   the business cycle

    B. expansion   D.   economic madness

2. GDP, CPI, unemployment rate and the national debt are all what?

    A. signs that the economy is peaking

    B. signs that the economy is in contraction

    C. economic indicators used to determine the state and direction of the economy

    D. elements of monetary policy

3. The new president proposes an economic plan to Congress. In it, he/she calls for lower taxes and recommends several programs requiring government spending. The president's proposal reflects what?

    A. his/her monetary policy
    B. his/her fiscal policy
    C. his/her desire to reduce inflation
    D. his/her ability to control the Federal Reserve

4. The Federal Reserve comes to the conclusion that more money must be pumped into the economy in an effort to stimulate economic growth. Which of the following actions could the "Fed" take that would result in increasing the money supply?

    A. raise the discount rate
    B. raise the reserve requirement
    C. sell securities (bonds)
    D. buy securities (bonds)

5. What is the message of the above cartoon?

    A. The Federal Reserve has too much power.
    B. The Federal Reserve should do something to stimulate the economy.
    C. US citizens should buy more bonds.
    D. The US Fiscal policy is working better than its monetary policy.

6. Margaret needs a new outfit for a party. She goes to a fashionable store where she has not shopped in over a year. Once there, she is surprised to find that a dress comparable to the one she bought the year before is almost $100 more than what she paid the last time she shopped there. Margaret is feeling the affects of

    A. recession.
    B. high taxes.
    C. inflation.
    D. stagflation.

7. The country of Zanbar has a national budget for the year 2006 of $15 billion. However, due to the outbreak of a war and some unexpected natural disasters, the government spends a total of $21 billion dollars by year's end. As a result, Zanbar has
   A. a national debt of $21 billion.
   B. experienced an increase in its national deficit but a decrease in its national debt.
   C. a national deficit for the year of $6 billion.
   D. a national debt for 2006 of $6 billion.

8. Increased consumption is a side-effect of
   A. higher taxes.
   B. higher interest rates.
   C. an easy money policy by the Federal Reserve.
   D. an increase in the discount rate by the Fed.

9. The overall supply of goods in an economy is known as
   A. overall goods.
   B. aggregate supply.
   C. open market supply.
   D. aggregate produce.

10. When the Federal Reserve lowers the discount rate
   A. interest rates rise.
   B. interest rates fall as well
   C. banks loan less money.
   D. people save more.

Chapter 4
The International Economy

SSEIN1	The student will explain why limited productive resources and unlimited wants result in scarcity, opportunity costs, and trade-offs for individuals, businesses, and governments.
SSEIN2	The student will give examples of how rational decision making entails comparing the marginal benefits and the marginal costs of an action.
SSEIN3	The student will explain how specialization and voluntary exchange between buyers and sellers increase the satisfaction of both parties.

4.1 INTERNATIONAL ECONOMIC CONCEPTS

International economics is the study of how economies in different countries and regions of the world interact and affect one another. International trade, market advantages, and international exchange rates are each important aspects of international economics. In this chapter, we will examine the importance of all three.

INTERNATIONAL TRADE

International trade is the buying and selling of goods and services across national borders. It is the process of nations exchanging goods with one another. No country produces everything it needs on its own. Therefore, all nations engage in some degree of international trade. **Exports** are goods that a nation sells to other countries. **Imports** are those goods that a nation buys from other countries.

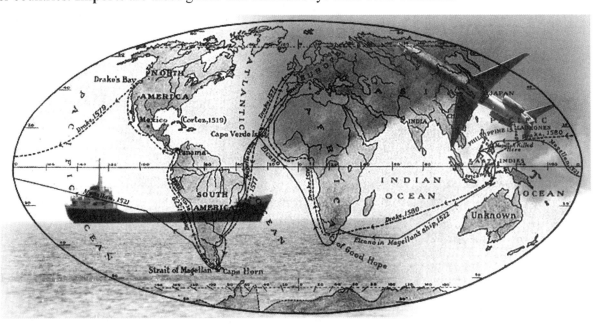

MARKET ADVANTAGES

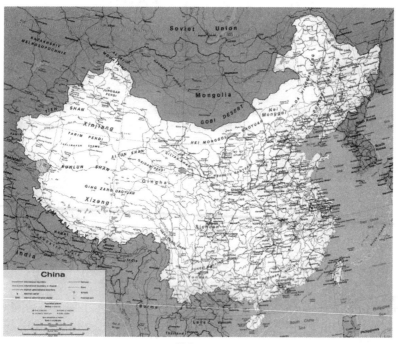

China

Several factors influence trade between countries. **Market advantages** occur when one country has an abundance of resources and/or can produce certain products more efficiently and in greater quantity than a competing nation. When studying why nations trade with one another, it is important to understand the difference between *absolute advantage* and *comparative advantage*. **Absolute advantage** means that a country can produce a product using less resources than another country. For example, if one person in China produces 80 units of rice or 20 units of tea, while in Russia one person produces 50 units of rice or 75 units of tea, then China has an absolute advantage in producing rice and Russia has an absolute advantage in producing tea. Why? China can produce more rice than Russia while Russia produces more tea than China. The country that can produce more, more efficiently, has the absolute advantage.

Comparative advantage, on the other hand, is different. A nation has a comparative advantage when it can produce a good at a lower *opportunity cost* than another nation. Remember that an **opportunity cost** is what a person, business, or government gives up when it chooses to allocate its resources one way instead of another. In some situations, there might be a country that can do a better job producing just about anything than the nation with which it trades. However, in order to focus on producing the goods it is *most* efficient at, it still finds it in its best interest to import certain products rather than producing them itself. For example, say that country X can produce 100 bags of wheat for every 1 bag country Y produces. At the same time, country X can also produce 2 boxes of fruit for every 1 that country Y produces. X can produce both products in greater numbers and more efficiently. However, in order to focus on its wheat production, it still decides to import fruit from country Y, because Y does almost as good a job as X at producing that particular good. Although country Y cannot produce as much fruit as X, it can produce fruit at a lower opportunity cost. Therefore, *comparatively*, it has an advantage. This is a crude example of how comparative advantage works; but hopefully it helps you understand the principle. In reality, the majority of international trade is based on comparative advantage because it benefits most countries in the long run.

Comparative Advantage

	Country X		Country Y		
Wheat	100 bags		1 bag	=	absolute advantage for X
	or			or	
Fruit	100 boxes		50 boxes	=	comparative advantage for Y

Practice 4.1 International Economic Concepts

1. When different countries exchange goods with one another, it is referred to as

   A. international trade.   C. comparative advantage.

   B. world-wide exchange rate.   D. market advantage.

2. Describe the difference between *absolute advantage* and *comparative advantage* when it comes to international economics.

4.2 TRADE RESTRICTIONS AND BARRIERS

FREE TRADE

Free trade is international trade without government restrictions. Some people support free trade while others oppose it. In the US, for example, some opponents of free trade argue that it hurts poor workers while helping only rich business owners. They claim that free trade encourages firms to move their plants and operations to countries where labor costs are lower. Others oppose free trade because they believe that it is bad for poor countries that are unable to compete as well in the global marketplace. Still, other groups oppose free trade because they believe it forces less economically developed countries to abandon their own traditions and cultures in favor of adopting a more westernized culture in an effort to compete economically. Finally, there have also been historical examples of producers exporting so much of a nation's crucial resource (i.e., food) on the international market that citizens at home have often suffered the effects of shortages. Supporters of free trade, however, claim that it creates jobs for the unemployed, promotes political freedom, and provides poorer countries with a chance to grow economically. In addition, consumers benefit from lower priced imported goods which also drive down the price of domestic goods and result in consumers' currency possessing more purchasing power (they can buy more). In September

2005, US Treasury Secretary John Snow supported free trade by insisting that "the removal of trade barriers is the greatest step the government can take to generate increased growth and poverty reductions."

GOVERNMENT-REGULATED TRADE

In reality, all countries have some degree of restrictions on international trade. Governments often intervene to regulate trade in an effort to help their nation's own businesses, increase jobs, help the national economy, or even to punish another nation economically. The most common types of trade restrictions are *quotas*, *tariffs*, *embargoes*, *standards*, and *subsidies*.

Government Regulated Trade

QUOTAS AND TARIFFS

A **quota** is a limitation on the number of units or the amount of a particular good that can be imported into a country. The US, for example, might only allow a certain amount of Canadian lumber to enter the US each year. Quotas limit competition by restricting the number of foreign products on the market. By comparison, **tariffs** are special taxes placed on products imported from another country. Governments sometimes use tariffs to raise the price of foreign goods and make domestic products more competitive in the marketplace. In the United States, labor unions have traditionally favored tariffs because they help US manufacturers and tend to protect jobs. Some US businesses, however, oppose tariffs because other countries tend to respond with tariffs of their own. Such tariffs make it more costly for US producers to sell their own goods abroad. Governments use both tariffs and quotas in an attempt to make domestic businesses more competitive so that they can increase their profits and, hopefully, contribute to a stronger economy. It is important to remember, however, that tariffs and quotas also limit competition by making it harder for foreign products to enter the marketplace. This keeps prices up and makes consumers less inclined to spend. As a result, tariffs can lower profits, raise unemployment, and ultimately hurt the economy if left in place for extended periods.

EMBARGOES

70's Gas Lines

Governments also use *embargoes* to impact trade. An **embargo** is when a country, or several countries, impose economic sanctions against a nation by refusing to trade with it. For instance, in 1973, US citizens found themselves waiting in long lines just to obtain gas for their cars because countries in the Middle East imposed an oil embargo against the United States. In 1979, the United States stopped shipping grain to the USSR after the Soviets invaded Afghanistan. Most notably, the United States has had a total economic embargo against the communist nation of Cuba for over forty years. No Cuban products can be legally shipped to or sold in the United States. Despite any demand that might exist in the marketplace, embargoes prohibit certain nations from trading with one another.

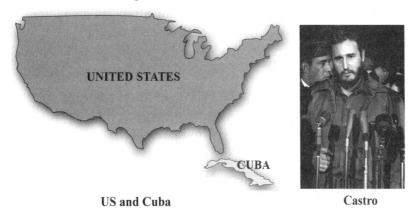

US and Cuba   Castro

STANDARDS

Food and Drug Administration Logo

Standards are another means of regulating trade. Standards are specific guidelines on goods coming into a country. For instance, before foreign products can enter and be sold in the United States, they must meet certain safety and health guidelines. Often, products that are traded internationally have to meet more restrictive standards in the nation they are shipped to than they would if they were sold at home.

Sometimes, however, businesses in a country with high safety or public health standards may lower their standards when they ship products to a nation where the standards are lower. They do this because it saves them money. Having to adhere to strict standards means that companies have to pay more money to make sure their products meet the necessary guidelines.

Although imposing high standards is often an effective way of protecting consumers, sometimes products traded internationally find their way into the marketplace despite failing to meet the required guidelines. For example, in 2007, as the United States continues to import more and more goods from China, a number of **recalls** on Chinese-made products had to be issued because these products failed to meet US safety and/or health standards. (A recall is when a manufacturer is forced to buy back a product, usually because it has been discovered to be unsafe.) A number of cats in the United States

Product: Emergency Tool Kits
Hazard: fire and shock

Product: Iced Tea Maker
Hazard: fire

Product: Various Children's Toys
Hazard: lead paint

Chinese Recall

died as the result of contaminated pet food shipped from China. Even more concerning, large numbers of toys were recalled once it was discovered that they contained lead-based paint (lead-based paint is poisonous for children). Such recalls are evidence that nations must not only put in place standards governing the products imported from other countries, they must work hard to enforce and monitor compliance to such standards as well.

SUBSIDIES

One reason countries don't like putting up trade barriers is that other countries are more likely to respond with trade barriers of their own. Therefore, countries will sometimes use *subsidies* to protect their domestic firms instead. A **subsidy** is a payment from the government to businesses. Subsidies redistribute income from the general taxpaying public to non-competitive firms, thereby helping the firms compete with foreign producers. Say, for example, that textile manufacturers in the US have to pay their employees a minimum wage. Textile manufacturers in India, however, do not have to pay such a wage. As a result, production cost Indian manufacturers a lot less money and, therefore, Indian companies can charge less for their product in the marketplace than US manufacturers. How can the

Business

US government protect the US manufacturers and keep them in business? One way is through the barriers and regulations we have already discussed. However, the government could also pay US manufacturers a subsidy. Because they receive a subsidy, these companies can now compete even though their costs of production are much higher. Subsidies also enable nations to protect their domestic industries without putting trade barriers in place.

The main drawback to subsidies is that they usually require higher taxes. The government uses tax money to support less efficient domestic industries or industries that are considered vital. If not subsidized, these industries might not make enough profit to continue supplying their product. Take, for example, public education. By paying up to 80% of the cost of tuition for in-state students to attend public universities, states encourage more of their citizens to get a college degree than otherwise might be able to if the cost of going to college was left solely to

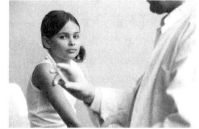
Vaccinations

the demands of the marketplace. Vaccinations are another example. Health agencies that offer immunizations against serious diseases are often subsidized to allow lower-income individuals who might otherwise not be able to afford certain vaccines to be immunized. Many economists argue that, if left to the natural forces of the marketplace, everything would eventually be produced more efficiently and priced so as to meet demand. Advocates of government subsidies, however, argue that to wait on such adjustments would hurt society too much in the short-term. They claim that the lack of subsidies would exclude too many people who could not initially afford goods and services that are in great demand (i.e., vaccines and a college education) but are priced high.

UGA

REASONS FOR TRADE BARRIERS

There are several reasons why governments enforce trade barriers. One of the most common is *protectionism* (putting policies in place that are designed to protect domestic industries from too much foreign competition). By restricting the importation of certain products or imposing tariffs, a government makes it more costly for domestic merchants to sell or for households and businesses to purchase foreign goods. This makes domestic products more attractive to consumers. As a result, people buy more domestic products, which helps domestic businesses increase their profits. In addition to ensuring that businesses do well, protectionism is also meant to create and protect domestic jobs. By enabling domestic businesses to be more profitable, barriers are meant to help increase the need for domestic workers.

National Security

National security is another reason why nations use trade barriers. Take, for instance, military weapons. If a nation is importing a large amount of its weapons, then that nation becomes largely dependent on the exporting nation for its national security. For this reason, countries which can produce their own military goods (i.e., the United States) tend to produce most of their military supplies at home. Otherwise, much needed military supplies could get cut off in a time of war. Meanwhile, during times of peace, nations that rely on other countries for military goods often have to appease the nations supplying them in order to get necessary military supplies. For example, because the US supplies a number of nations with military weapons, these nations have to strongly consider the wishes of the United States in both their international and domestic decisions. If they don't, the US could stop exporting military goods such nations desperately depend on. Preventing trade in illegal goods (i.e., drugs and illegal weapons) and in materials that could be used for harmful purposes (i.e., chemicals or parts that could be used by terrorists to manufacture a bomb) are other forms of trade restriction designed to protect national security.

Governments will also restrict trade in order to protect citizens' **health**. As mentioned earlier when we discussed how standards impact trade, different nations will require that imported products meet with certain guidelines before they can enter the country. In the United States, there are a number of agencies which make sure that food, drugs, and various other products meet US standards before they can be sold legally in the US.

Finally, nations might enforce trade barriers out of **retaliation**. For example, let's say that the United States thinks that the best policy is to engage in free trade. It doesn't want any trade barriers. However, it soon discovers that its products in India are suffering because India's government is imposing high tariffs on US imported goods. Meanwhile, the same Indian companies who are being protected at home by these tariffs are selling their exported goods in the United States without having to pay any tariffs themselves. The Indian manufacturers are enjoying an unfair advantage over US manufacturers who make the same product. Therefore, since the US government has no authority to do away with India's tariffs, it responds the only way it can: with tariffs of its own. By enforcing a trade barrier (a new US tariff) the United States government seeks to make its own firms more competitive.

Embargoes (mentioned earlier) are another form of economic retaliation. Although they are an economic action, embargoes are normally put in place for political reasons. Refusing to trade with a government that violates its citizens' civil rights, refuses to stop manufacturing nuclear weapons, has invaded a weaker country, or is guilty of violating some international law are all examples of reasons nations impose embargoes. Embargoes are intended to make a country change its political, social, or military policies by applying economic pressure.

COSTS AND BENEFITS OF TRADE BARRIERS

Fashion

There are several **benefits to trade barriers**. Barriers help domestic businesses compete at home, can often serve to protect domestic jobs, maintain standards of safety in the marketplace, and help poorer nations that are still trying to develop economically and compete with wealthier nations on the international market. (Any industries trying to establish themselves in a developing country would likely fail if forced to compete directly against businesses exporting from more developed nations if the market were totally open to free trade.) However, there are **costs to trade barriers** as well. For instance, barriers tend to limit the number of goods in the marketplace because it is harder for foreign manufacturers to sell their products. Even those foreign products that do reach the market are often priced higher because of the additional standards they have to meet or tariffs that are required. All this affects consumers. When supply is limited and consumers have fewer choices, prices go up. In addition, when manufacturers have to pay tariffs, this raises prices on foreign products which allows domestic manufacturers to keep their prices high as well. In short, trade barriers usually result in people having to pay more for the things they want. Also, while trade barriers often help businesses that sell goods at home, they tend to hurt businesses that trade overseas. Why? When a nation imposes tariffs on imported goods, it often encourages other nations to impose tariffs as well (remember the example of the US and India mentioned above?). Therefore, a manufacturer shipping their products overseas often has a harder time making a profit in the process. Also, just as barriers can protect US citizens, they can also prove harmful as well. For example, one of the main concerns facing citizens today is the rising price of prescription drugs. Drugs manufactured in the US are often very expensive and many people who need them have a hard time affording them. In addition, because of the US' strict standards, drugs that are available quickly in other nations are often not available for years in the US because of all the testing that is required. As a result, many US citizens want the freedom to order their drugs from nations like Canada. The US, however, has tight restrictions on importing prescription drugs. Many of the prescription drugs people want cannot be legally imported. As a result, many citizens continue to pay more than they can afford for medicines or break the law by obtaining their drugs illegally.

INTERNATIONAL ORGANIZATIONS AND AGREEMENTS

There are several organizations that exist to facilitate international trade and a number of agreements in place to help regulate its practice. Below are just a few examples.

World Trade Organization (WTO)	International organization that establishes rules for international trade and helps resolve disputes between member nations. **World Trade Organization**
European Union (EU)	Trading union consisting of 25 European nations that facilitates trade and commerce as it seeks to create a unified regional, rather than national, economy.
Association of Southeast Asian Nations (ASEAN)	International organization that aims to accelerate economic growth, social progress, and cultural development among its members.

United Nations (UN)	International diplomatic body centered in New York City. Its member nations seek to engage in diplomacy to deal with international issues. In addition to potential military conflicts, it also seeks effective solutions to economic matters as well. Its ability to provide workable solutions and negotiate peaceful resolutions to armed conflicts helps determine how the worldwide economy responds to international circumstances.  **United Nations**
North American Free Trade Agreement (NAFTA)	Trade agreement ratified during the Clinton administration, which lowered trade barriers between the US, Canada, and Mexico. It caused concerns in the US as some feared it would result in the loss of US jobs. Proponents of the agreement argued, however, that NAFTA would benefit the economy by allowing US businesses greater access to foreign markets.  **NAFTA Signing**

BALANCE OF TRADE AND BALANCE OF PAYMENTS

The rate at which a nation trades with other nations is called its **balance of trade.** A nation's balance of trade can be either *favorable* or *unfavorable*. A **favorable balance of trade** is when a country exports more than it imports (brings money into the economy). An **unfavorable balance of trade** is when a nation imports more than it exports. By comparison, a nation's **balance of**

payments is the value of all money coming into the country thanks to exports minus all of the money going out of the country as it pays for imports (review our discussion of net exports in chapter 3 under section 3.1). Balance of payments is divided into two areas: *current* and *capital accounts*. The current account includes the trade in goods and services while the capital account includes foreign investments. For many years, the US has run a current account deficit which has been balanced by a capital account surplus. In other words, the US has had trade deficits that it is able to finance because foreigners have invested their funds in the United States. If it were not for this large financial investment in US securities and financial institutions, the US would not have the foreign currency to run a trade deficit.

US-Japan Trade

Just in case you are having trouble understanding the relationship between current and capital accounts, let's look at the example of the United States and Japan. The US buys more goods from Japan than Japan does from the US. Therefore, Japan has an excess of American dollars. It's making more money off of exporting goods to the United States than the US makes off of exporting goods to Japan. However, Japan invests much of this money back into the United States by purchasing office buildings, golf courses, factories, and other types of property. This pumps money back into the US economy and is a prime example of balance of payments at work.

Practice 4.2 Trade Restrictions and Barriers

1. Taxes imposed on imports are called

    A. subsidies.   B. tariffs.   C. embargoes.   D. standards.

2. How would someone who wanted to see all trade barriers removed have felt about NAFTA?
    A. they would have opposed it on the grounds that it would cost too many US jobs.
    B. they would have supported it because it called for subsidies.
    C. they would have opposed it on the grounds that it made tariffs too high.
    D. they would have supported it for establishing free trade.

3. What are trade barriers? What are some of the costs and benefits to a country that institutes trade barriers?

4. What is the difference between *balance of trade* and *balance of payments*? Describe what is meant by *current account* and *capital account*.

4.3 PURCHASING POWER AND EXCHANGE RATES

Since countries tend to measure money differently, it is important to know how much the currency in one nation is worth in another nation. After all, if you're a US citizen and want to open a business in Japan, then you better know how many US dollars comprise one Japanese yen. How much the primary form of currency in one nation is worth in comparison to the primary form of currency in another nation is called the **exchange rate**. Exchange rates are important among international trade because they decide how much money must transfer between countries in order to complete a trade or purchase. For example, if a chair is made in China or a bowl is made in France, then an importer probably had to pay for it in Chinese yuan or European euros. How does a US importer get Chinese or European currency with which to pay for these products? They *exchange* US dollars for the equivalent worth in the Chinese or European currency. As you can see, it is important for businesses that deal internationally (and citizens who travel internationally, for that matter) to be aware of the exchange rate.

DETERMINING EXCHANGE RATES

There are three types of exchange rate. First, a rate of exchange may be fixed. **Fixed exchange rates** establish a price for a foreign currency that is tied to a stable currency of a developed country. These currencies are often called hard currencies. The US dollar, the European euro, and the British pound, are all examples of hard currencies. For instance, China, Belize, and Panama are countries with exchange rates set at a fixed value with respect to the US dollar. In these countries, the central bank acts to ensure that one of the local currencies equals a fixed number of US dollars. As the value of the US dollar rises and falls, so does the currency in these countries. Fixed exchange rates allow less developed nations to tie their currency to the more stable currency of a developed country. They do this to assure potential investors of their currency's stability, thereby encouraging more investment in their economy.

Globe

Secondly, there is what's known as a *floating exchange rate*. A **floating exchange rate** is determined by supply and demand. The United States, Japan, Canada, Romania, and Bulgaria are examples of nations with floating exchange rates. Consider the value of the US dollar in terms of the Japanese yen. The supply of US dollars in Japan depends upon the demand by US citizens for Japanese goods like cars and electronic goods. In other words, Japan gets dollars by selling goods to the United States. If the demand for dollars increases or decreases it will effect the exchange rate value. Demand for dollars is largely synonymous with demand for US products because foreigners mostly purchase dollars to buy US goods. Therefore, increased demand for US products causes the demand for dollars to shift to the right in the diagram labeled *Floating Exchange Rate Diagram*, while lack of demand for US products causes the demand curve to shift left.

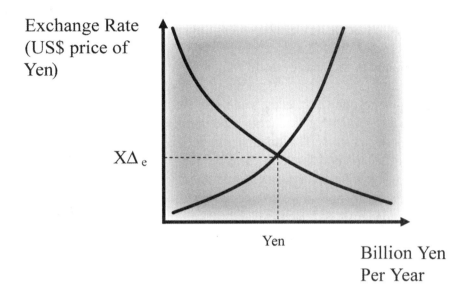

The final type of exchange rate is a *managed floating exchange rate*. A **managed floating** exchange rate floats within an agreed upon band, but if the value gets above or below a certain value, the central bank intervenes. If the value gets too low, the central bank will reduce the supply

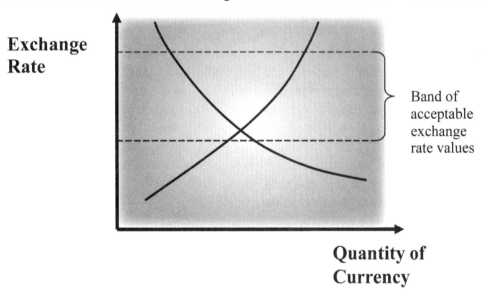

of currency to bring the value back up. If the value gets too high, the central bank will increase the supply to get the value back down. China, Greece, Hungary, Israel, and Turkey are some of the nations with managed floating exchange rates.

CURRENCY APPRECIATION AND DEPRECIATION

When the value of currency becomes greater, it is said to have appreciated. **Currency appreciation** benefits consumers but can be a bad thing for producers. When the value of a nation's currency appreciates, consumers in that country can buy more foreign products. For example, when the dollar increases in value from equalling a certain amount of Mexican pesos to equaling even more, US citizens can afford to buy more Mexican goods even though the amount of money they have is the same. However, currency appreciation also means that producers' products become more expensive for foreign customers. While the average US consumer might be thrilled to know that they can buy more Mexican products for fewer dollars, US businesses that want to sell their goods in Mexico City are now more discouraged. This is because it now takes more pesos to afford the US products. Since Mexican customers want to pay as little as possible for the product, they are less likely to buy from US businesses and more likely to

International Currency

buy from another country instead. Because high appreciation can hurt demand for a country's exports, nations generally don't want their currency to appreciate too much. Sometimes, in order to reverse a trade deficit, a nation will voluntarily devalue its currency (make it worth less). Lowering a nation's currency value on purpose is called *devaluation*. By devaluing its currency, a nation makes it easier for people in other countries to buy its products, thereby resulting in more exports.

The opposite of currency appreciation is **currency depreciation**. A depreciating currency decreases in value. Depreciation's effects are the very opposite of appreciation. Exporters in a country with depreciating currency are better off because more foreign buyers will purchase their products. However, consumers in the same country now cannot buy as many foreign products as they once could. Suppose the US dollar drops below the Japanese yen in value. US consumers are now hurting because their dollar buys less Japanese product than it use to. They now have to pay more for Japanese cars and electronic equipment. However, US producers who export to Japan are happy because their products are now cheaper on the Japanese market. The lower prices mean that Japanese consumers will buy more US goods. In short, then, currency depreciation is good for producers but bad for consumers in the same country.

Below is a table depicting exchange rates in different nations compared to the US dollar for the years 2001 through 2006. Examine the table and see if you can answer the questions that follow.

EXCHANGE RATE TABLE				
YEAR	U.S. DOLLAR ($)	JAPANESE YEN (¥)	BRITISH POUND (£)	FRENCH EURO (€)
2001	1	121.5	.69	7.3
2002	1	125.4	.67	6.9
2003	1	115.9	.61	5.8
2004	1	108.2	.55	5.2
2005	1	110.2	.55	5.2
2006	1	116.3	.54	5.2

1. In 2002, the US dollar was worth more than the standard currency of which country/countries?

   A. Japan
   B. Great Britain
   C. France
   D. Japan, Great Britain, and France
   E. France and Japan
   F. Great Britain and Japan

2. From 2001 to 2006, the value of the Japanese yen has _____ compared to the US dollar.

   A. appreciated
   B. depreciated
   C. remained stable

(Answers: 1. E, 2. A)

FACTORS AFFECTING EXCHANGE RATES

Productivity

What factors affect the demand for a nation's currency? One key factor is a country's **interest rates** on investments. If, for example, the United States' interest rate increases relative to that of other countries, the demand for US dollars will increase. Foreign investors will want to invest in US securities in order to collect the high interest. Provided that there is not a sudden increase in the supply of dollars on the foreign exchange market, the increased demand for dollars will cause the dollar to appreciate (kind of like how the price of products increase when they are in high demand). A second important factor is **productivity**. As you know by now, productivity is the amount of goods that a nation is producing. As a nation's productivity increases relative to the rest of the world, so does the demand for its currency. Third, demand for currency is affected by **consumer tastes**. If foreign consumers begin to prefer US goods more than goods from other countries, then demand for US dollars will rise. Finally, **economic stability** greatly affects the value of currency. The more stable an economy is, the more foreign investors demand its currency. Of course, the reverse of these changes will cause demand for a currency to decrease and depreciation will occur.

PURCHASING POWER

The appreciation and depreciation of currency affect *purchasing power*. **Purchasing power** is the actual amount of goods and services that can be bought with a given unit of money. In other words, the purchasing power of a dollar is determined by how much one dollar will buy. **Purchasing power parity** is when the same product sells for the same amount of currency in different countries. In other words, a Coke that costs $1 in the United States would cost $1 worth of yen in Japan, $1 worth of pesos in Mexico, $1 worth of pounds in London, and so on, and so on. In reality, however, purchasing power parity rarely occurs. This is due to a number of factors. Whether or not a nation is experiencing a growing or shrinking economy, inflation, unemployment levels, government regulations, etc. can all influence supply and demand and determine what amount of money producers can charge in one nation for their product versus what they can charge in another. The graph below, for example, shows the price of a Big Mac™ in a number of countries around the world in US dollars at the market exchange rate, and the exchange rate in terms of purchasing power parity.

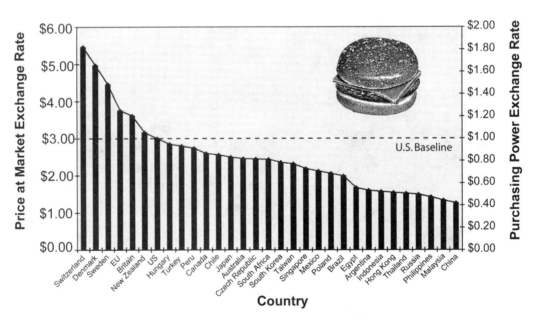

Purchasing Power and the Big Mac Index

Practice 4.3 Purchasing Power and Exchange Rate

1. The term *exchange rate* refers to

    A.   how much interest one nation offers on investments.
    B.   how much one nation's form of currency is worth compared to another nation's currency.
    C.   the amount of goods a unit of currency will buy.
    D.   the degree of demand for one nation's exports in another country.

2. An appreciating currency in Canada benefits

    A.   consumers in other countries who want to purchase Canadian products.
    B.   Canadian producers.
    C.   foreign consumers of Canadian goods.
    D.   Canadian consumers.

3. Explain the difference between a fixed exchange rate, floating exchange rate, and managed floating exchange rate.

CHAPTER 4 REVIEW

Key terms and concepts

imports

exports

market advantages

absolute advantage

comparitive advantage

quota

tariffs

embargo

standards

subsidy

protectionism

free trade

benefits to trade barriers

costs of trade barriers

European Union (EU)

Association of Southeast Asian Nations (ASEAN)

North American Free Trade Agreement (NAFTA)

balance of trade

favorable balance of trade

unfavorable balance of trade

balance of payments

exchange rate

fixed exchange rate

floating exchange rate

managed floating

currency appreciation

currency depreciation

factors affecting exchange rates

purchasing power

purchasing power parity

Multiple Choice Questions:

1. France imports more products from China than China imports from France. In this scenario, France has

    A. a favorable balance of trade with China.
    B. an unfavorable balance of trade with China.
    C. an advantage in net exports.
    D. a comparative advantage.

2. The fact that the US tends to import goods from Guatemala that it could produce more abundantly itself tends to suggest that

    A. Guatemala has a comparative advantage in producing these goods.
    B. Guatemala enjoys an absolute advantage in producing these goods.
    C. Guatemala has more net exports than the US.
    D. Guatemala enjoys a current account surplus over the US.

3. Which of the following parties would be most likely to favor US tariffs?

    A. producers of exported US products.

    B. US consumers.

    C. US labor unions.

    D. foreign producers of US imports.

4. The international community has just discovered that the leaders of the nation of Simgowa are executing large numbers of citizens who it accuses of opposing the government. In an effort to put economic pressure on Simgowa to stop these mass murders, the international community refuses to ship food and military weapons to the country, while refusing to buy Simgowa's products. As a result, Simgowa ceases its brutal actions and asks other nations to resume trade relations. Simgowa has responded to

    A. tariffs.   C. international standards.

    B. an embargo.   D. international subsidies.

5. Which of the following can limit the availability of foreign products?

    A. product standards   C. lack of quotas

    B. free trade   D. few domestic subsidies

6. When the US dollar appreciates, US consumers can

    A. afford to buy fewer foreign products.

    B. afford to buy more foreign products.

    C. have to pay higher tariffs.

    D. impose more quotas.

7. The nation of Anturmo is still struggling to develop economically. It depends on help from other nations and is trying desperately to encourage foreign investment in its economy. It sounds like Anturmo would benefit most from

    A. a fixed exchange rate.   C. a managed floating exchange rate.

    B. a floating exchange rate.   D. no exchange rate.

8. Brian is the CEO of a US company that depends on profits from exports overseas for the bulk of its business. Brian would most like to see

    A. the dollar appreciate.   C. more foreign tariffs.

    B. more US tariffs.   D. the dollar depreciate.

Chapter 5
Personal Finance Economics

SSEPF1	The student will explain why limited productive resources and unlimited wants result in scarcity, opportunity costs, and trade-offs for individuals, businesses, and governments.
SSEPF2	The student will give examples of how rational decision making entails comparing the marginal benefits and the marginal costs of an action.
SSEPF3	The student will explain how specialization and voluntary exchange between buyers and sellers increase the satisfaction of both parties.
SSEPF4	The student will compare and contrast different economic systems and explain how they answer the three basic economic questions of what to produce, how to produce, and for whom to produce.
SSEPF5	The student will describe the roles of government in a market economy.
SSEPF6	The student will explain how productivity, economic growth, and future standards of living are influenced by investment in factories, machinery, new technology, and the health, education, and training of people.

5.1 RATIONAL DECISION MAKING

INCENTIVES

People are motivated by *incentives*. An incentive is any factor, goal, ambition, etc. that leads someone to act in a particular way. A **positive incentive** is a reward that a person is likely to receive if they behave in a certain manner. For example, if Joe is promised a 10% raise if he sells eighty pairs of shoes this month, then Joe has a *positive incentive* to sell shoes. The fact that he will make more money is a positive consequence of doing a good job. By contrast, a **negative incentive** is a punishment or negative consequence that one wants to avoid for failing to behave in a certain manner. If Joe is told that he will be fired if he fails to sell eighty pairs of shoes this month, then Joe has a *negative incentive* to sell shoes. Being fired is a negative consequence that Joe desperately wants to avoid. People and businesses tend to respond to positive and negative consequences in predictable ways. Households, businesses, and even governments, are motivated to behave in a fashion that rewards them economically (i.e.,increased income, profits, or revenue), while avoiding behavior that will hurt them economically (i.e., less income, fewer profits, less revenue).

Job Reward

Unemployed

ANOTHER LOOK AT THE RATIONAL DECISION MAKING MODEL

Einstein

In chapter 1, we looked at a **rational decision making model** for making economic decisions (remember Tom's date with Melissa at the football game?). Although that example hopefully did a good job of demonstrating how people make rational decisions, the concept is important enough that it's worth a second look. As mentioned before, when people make economic decisions, they go through (whether consciously or unconsciously) a rational decision-making process. Let's review the steps:

1. **DEFINE THE PROBLEM:** Since money is scarce, people often can't afford to spend it on everything they would like. Therefore, they have to choose one option over another.

2. **LIST THE ALTERNATIVES:** Given the fact that you can't afford everything, what are your realistic choices?

3. **STATE THE CRITERIA:** What is most important to you? What is your main incentive? Understanding what motivates you will help you make the wisest decision. (For Tom in chapter 1, his top priority was pleasing and getting a second date with Melissa.)

4. **EVALUATE THE ALTERNATIVES:** Determine which choice comes closest to helping you get what is most important to you. (Again, in Tom's case, buying Melissa the food and drink she wanted was the best alternative based on his criteria.)

5. **MAKE A RATIONAL DECISION:** The rational decision is to choose the alternative that best meets your criteria. After all, it wouldn't make much sense to determine that option B does the most to provide you with the result you want, then choose option A.

Sports Car

Before we move on, let's look at one more example of this decision making model in action. Rikki is just about to finish high school. Before graduation, her parents tell her that, since the time she was just a little girl, they have been saving money to give her when she graduates. Rikki learns that, upon graduation, she will receive $50,000. Rikki must now decide between: A) using the money to pay for college and continuing to drive her old, used car; or B) using the money to buy the awesome new sports car she desperately wants, then working her way through college.

1. ***Rikki's problem:*** She does not have enough money for both the sports car and full tuition to college.

2. Rikki's alternatives:

   alternative 1 -- She can use the money to pay full tuition, avoid having to work while in school, and continue to drive the old, used car. But this will mean giving up the thrill of driving a brand new sports car.

   alternative 2 -- She can buy the sports car. However, she will have no money left for college and will have to work to afford tuition. This will make college much harder and will likely mean that it takes her longer to graduate.

   alternative 3 -- She can buy the sports car, go to work, and forget about college all together. This will still allow her to have the car she wants and will be much easier than trying to work and go to school at the same time. However, she will miss out on going to college and will likely have a difficult time getting the high-paying job she's always dreamed of without a college degree.

   alternative 4 -- She can use part of the money for a down payment on the car and part of it for tuition. This way she can go ahead and get the car, while still having some left over for college. She will not have to work as much to pay for school, but she will still have to work some and will also have to make monthly car payments with interest.

   alternative 5 -- She can use the money to buy the car and take out a student loan for tuition. This will allow her to have the car and she will not have to work while she is in school. However, she will have several thousands of dollars in debt when she graduates because she will have to pay the loan back with interest.

3. ***What is Rikki's criteria:*** After much consideration, Rikki decides that the most important thing to her is to have long-term financial security. She wants to know that, for years to come, she will have plenty of money to live comfortably and do the things she wants.

4. ***Evaluating Rikki's alternatives:*** Rikki carefully evaluates each alternative. If she buys the car, she will experience the immediate gratification of having a fun new sports car to drive. However, she will have a much harder time in school which will likely mean it takes longer to graduate and could affect her grades. Lower grades could make it harder for her to get the job she wants when she graduates. A less attractive job could likely mean less pay, making it harder for Rikki to live the way she wants to. Meanwhile, the idea of having to make car payments before she even graduates or going into debt to pay for college seems to work against her goal of getting off to a good start financially once she's out of school. Finally, the idea of skipping college all together is out of the question because Rikki knows that almost any job providing the kind of financial security she wants will require a college degree.

5. ***Rikki's rational economic decision:*** After considering each options trade-offs and opportunity costs (see rational decision making model example in chapter 1), Rikki decides that the best decision is to hold off on the car, keep driving what she's driving for now, and spend the money on college. This will allow her to focus entirely on school, make the best grades possible, become an attractive candidate for a high-paying job, and start her new life after college without debt. If she does all that, Rikki reasons that she will eventually be able to afford almost any car she wants anyway.

Once again, this simple example hopefully helps you understand how people make rational financial decisions.

Practice 5.1 Rational Decision Making

1. Bill's boss informs him that the firm he works for is going to be promoting someone to the position of vice president sometime in the next six months. Bill wants the job, so he works as hard as he can to impress his boss and bring in profits for the company. Bill is motivated by a

   A. rational decision.
   B. negative incentive.
   C. positive incentive.
   D. list of alternatives.

2. Describe what is meant by a *rational economic decision.*

5.2 HOW FINANCIAL INSTITUTIONS AND INVESTMENTS WORK

In general, people want to save and see their money grow. As a result, many citizens invest at least part of their money in either savings accounts through financial institutions, or some other form of investment. In this section, we'll look closer at how different financial institutions function and examine how personal investments work.

BANKS, CREDIT UNIONS, AND SAVINGS & LOANS

Bank of America-Charlotte. NC

Most US adults have financial accounts (savings accounts, checking accounts, etc.). Such accounts are usually held by a *commercial bank*, *credit union*, or a *savings and loan*. **Commercial banks** are financial institutions that receive deposits of money, extend credit, and provide loans. Commercial banks are similar to corporations in that stockholders own and manage them in order to make a profit. Banks make money mostly through granting loans that charge interest. Meanwhile, the bank also pays interest to those who deposit money in one of the accounts the bank offers. The bank pays interest to the depositor in exchange for the depositor allowing the bank to use their money to finance other transactions and investments. Conversely, the bank also charges interest to anyone who borrows money from the bank. It is important to remember that banks and other financial institutions tend to pay less interest to depositors/investors than they charge borrowers. For those who deposit and borrow money from the bank, this means that their **interest charged** (interests the bank charges them to borrow) is greater than their **interest earned** (interest the bank pays them for the use of their money). Banks and other financial institutions must charge greater interest than they pay in order to make a profit. Say that Sally deposits $10,000 in Kennesaw Mountain Bank. Then, suppose Charlie borrows $10,000 from the same institution. If Kennesaw Mountain Bank pays more interest to Sally than it earns from Charlie, it will lose money. If it charges both the same interest, it will only break even and will still make no profit (thereby having no incentive to stay in business). But, if Kennesaw Mountain Bank charges Charlie greater interest than it pays Sally, then the bank makes money and can continue to operate and grow.

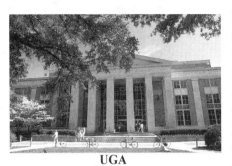
UGA

Banks commonly grant loans to individuals to buy houses (mortgages), purchase cars, start their own business, etc. Usually, before banks will grant loans to individuals or businesses, they require that they possess enough *collateral*. Collateral is anything of value that could be used to cover the value of the loan should one be unable to repay. For example, when you borrow money to buy a car, the car is collateral. If you don't pay, the bank can take the car and sell it. Another example is if you fail to pay your mortgage, the bank can foreclose and sell your house. Borrowers will often use their house as collateral for other kinds of loans as well. Often, parents will use their home as collateral to borrow money to pay for their kid's college education or to cover some huge expense. Requiring borrowers to have collateral is how financial institutions protect themselves against financial loss.

Credit unions are somewhat different from banks. They are cooperative associations that serve only their members. Like banks, they offer checking and savings accounts, as well as grant loans. However, because they are technically non-profits, credit unions do not have to pay the same taxes as commercial banks. This means that they can usually offer higher interest rates. Credit unions, however, are exclusive; only certain individuals may join. For instance, many states have state employee credit unions, which are open only to those who either are, or have been, employees of the state.

Credit Union

George Bailey

Finally, **savings and loan associations** are saving institutions designed to aid home building (in the classic Christmas movie, *It's a Wonderful Life,* George Bailey runs a savings and loan). Historically, savings and loans lend their money out as mortgages on homes. In the 1980s, many savings and loans made bad investments and ended up going bankrupt. Because they were not government insured at the time, taxpayers had to bear the burden of bailing them out. The bad taste left by the 80s, along with the fact that credit unions and commercial banks offer similar services, has caused a decline in the popularity of savings and loan associations.

RISK AND RETURN

People tend to invest when they are confident that the likely return of their investment is worth any risk. ***Return*** refers to the eventual payoff of the investment. For instance, a real estate developer may invest (spend) $500,000 building a condominium complex if he/she is confident they will eventually sell all the units for $2 million. ***Risk*** refers to the chance that an investment might actually end up losing money rather than making it. If an investor invests some of their money in a new business, there is a risk that the business might fail, costing the investor the money they invested. Often times, the riskiest investments are also the one's that offer the greatest possible return if they work. For this reason, some investors are still willing to make risky investments. The key is to determine how much risk one can afford. If you make a certain investment, will you still be OK financially if it fails and you lose what you invested? If so, then an investor might want to take the risk in hope of a profitable return. However, if, after considering the risk, you determine that you could not endure the financial blow you would suffer if the investment fails, it

Gambling

Risky Business

would be much wiser to pass on that investment and invest your money in something else that carries less risk.

STOCKS, BONDS, AND MUTUAL FUNDS

Bonds

As mentioned before, **stocks** are shares in a company that an individual/organization purchases giving that person/entity part ownership. People buy stocks hoping to see its value increase over time. In the 1950s, the American Family Life Assurance Company started in

Wall Street

Columbus, Georgia. Initially, its owners sold stock at a very low price to finance their new business. As a result, many people bought a good number of shares for only a few hundred dollars. Today, those who kept this initial stock in AFLAC have made millions. The problem with stocks is that they can be risky, and few people know enough to be "experts in the market". While it is great that those early investors in AFLAC did so well, investors in a corporation called Enron had a much different experience. Enron was a huge corporation that went bust after years of economic promise. As a result, many investors lost their money. Some even lost their life's savings! Since stocks can be risky, many investors put their money in *mutual funds* in order to minimize risks. **Mutual funds** pool money from a number of investors to buy a range of stocks. Thus, an investor's money is dispersed among several companies. This reduces risk because, if one company does poorly, others are likely doing better. Because they are generally managed by a financial expert, investors are free to focus on other things without having to constantly keep an eye on their investments. The downside to mutual funds is that they generally offer a lower rate of return and investors must pay part of what they earn to the financial fund manager. **Bonds**, as we learned earlier, are loans to either a company or the government. Unlike stocks, which make an investor part owner in a business, bonds are simply a loan from the investor. Bonds are another way people invest.

REASONS PEOPLE SAVE AND INVEST

Retirees

Why do citizens choose to save their money and invest in stocks, mutual funds, etc. rather than spend it? There are a number of reasons. As we've discussed earlier, people are inclined to save when interest rates are higher and invest when the potential return is likely to outweigh the loss of immediate gratification. Simply put, people save and invest because there is something they want in the future that is more important to them than anything they might purchase with the same money today. People save to buy a house, a car, take a vacation, purchase a luxury item, have their first baby, pay for their children's college education, etc. One of the biggest things people commonly save for is retirement. **Retirement** is when people stop working a paying job because they simply don't want to work anymore or because they are physically unable due to their age and/or health (age is the number one reason people retire.). Of course, since most people rely on their job for income, people who retire have to get money from somewhere else. For this reason, wise people begin saving while they are young so that they will have money when they retire. Many invest their money in stocks and mutual funds through retirement plans offered at their jobs. Others put money in IRAs (investment retirement accounts). Such saving allows people to put money aside that then grows with compound interest (we'll discuss compound interest more shortly). Then, when they retire, they can use it in place of the income once provided by their employment. (The government also provides retirement benefits through Social Security. However, the amount paid by this program continues to shrink and some wonder if it will even exist in fifty years. Wise citizens will be sure to come up with their own savings plans rather than relying on Social Security to provide the bulk of their retirement income.)

WORKERS' EARNINGS

Closely tied to investment and saving is the topic of **workers' earnings** (how much employers pay workers for their labor). Workers' earnings determine how much money laborers have to spend and save/invest for the future. How much money one is likely to make in the labor market due to their skills, training, education, etc., is called their **earning potential**. People who are financially successful tend to earn more money for their labor because they possess special skills and/or training. Usually, the highest paid workers are college educated, have good communication skills, know how to show proper respect to peers and authority figures, conduct themselves professionally, and have actively sought to improve their skills with additional training. For these reasons, individuals who want to get a good job and find a career that will allow them to live comfortably and save for the future need to invest their time and money in getting as much education and training as possible.

Workers

Practice 5.2   Financial Institutions and Investments

1. Describe the differences and similarities between banks and credit unions.

2. How are stocks and bonds different, and what is a mutual fund?

3. Francine wants to start her own hair salon. She goes to the bank and takes out a loan for $200,000. Meanwhile, Robert's new job has gone well and he is making a lot of money. He decides to deposit $100,000 in the same bank. The bank they both use will

    A. charge Francine higher interest than they pay Robert.
    B. pay Robert higher interest than they charge Francine.
    C. end up paying Robert exactly what they charge Francine because Robert deposited less money than Francine borrowed.
    D. require them both to be members of the bank before they can open an account or acquire a loan.

4. Using the information you've learned in section 5.1 and section 5.2, come up with a specific financial goal (i.e., paying for college, buying a house, retiring as a millionaire, etc.). Then, consult with your teacher and/or a group of classmates and come up with a savings and investment plan that can help you achieve it. What are some of the rational decisions you will have to make?

5.3 THE EFFECTS OF FISCAL AND MONETARY POLICY ON INDIVIDUALS

In chapter 3, we discussed fiscal and monetary policy. Specifically, we looked at how they affect the economy overall. Now, let's look more closely at how the government's fiscal and monetary policy impacts everyday citizens.

THE IMPACT OF FISCAL POLICY

Hopefully, you remember that fiscal policy refers to how the government chooses to tax and spend. How do such decisions affect individuals? Let's consider the following example.

Trent earns $60,000 per year. Let's say that, between the federal and state government, Trent pays $15,000 per year in taxes. That means that Trent has $45,000 a year left over. Because he is a responsible guy, Trent is determined to take his father's advice and save 10% of his overall income. Since 6,000 is 10% of $60,000 (Trent's overall income before taxes), Trent puts $3,000 into a savings account and another $3,000 into a 401k plan at work. That leaves Trent with $39,000 to spend in the economy. With that money he pays his rent, buys food and clothes, pays utilities, makes his car payment, spends money on leisure activities, etc.

Now, however, let's say that the government raises taxes while Trent's salary remains the same. Instead of $15,000 per year, Trent now must pay $20,000 per year. He now only has $40,000 per year left over. Because of his necessary expenses, Trent cannot quite afford to save a full 10% of his overall income, he can only afford to save about $4,000, meaning less money for the bank or businesses Trent would have invested in. This means that it may take Trent longer to save for a house or that he may have less money when he retires because he couldn't save as much. In addition, because of the higher tax rate, he does not have as much money left over to spend either. Therefore, Trent spends less money in the market place because he cannot purchase as many things. In short, the government's tax decisions affect average citizens whose actions, in turn, impact the entire economy.

However, let's not forget the other half of fiscal policy: spending. While Trent's finances may suffer somewhat from the higher taxes necessary to fund government programs, it is also possible that he may benefit from the programs themselves. For instance, his kids may get a cheaper education or more affordable health care. If he loses his job, he may receive unemployment benefits that allow him to survive until he gets a new one. His community might finally get the improved roads and additional police officers it needs, etc. Can you see now how fiscal policy affects average citizens?

PROGRESSIVE, REGRESSIVE, AND PROPORTIONAL TAXES

What *type* of taxes citizens pay is also important. A **progressive tax** is one in which the amount of tax one pays increases with income. In other words, if a nation or state used a progressive tax to tax income, then someone who makes $100,000 per year is responsible for paying a higher percentage of their income than someone who makes $35,000 per year. While the person earning $100,000 might have to pay 15% of their income in taxes ($15,000), the person making $35,000 might only have to pay 5% ($1750). By comparison, a **regressive tax** is one in which people pay a higher percentage of tax the *less* money they make. **Sales taxes** are a common example of a regressive tax because people with less money pay a higher percentage in tax. How so? Suppose Liss and Gerald both want to buy the same model television. Liss makes $65,000/year, while Gerald only makes $45,000. However, the price of the television is the same for both of them: $800. In addition, the sales tax on the TV is based on a percentage of the

Paying Taxes

television's price, not Liss and Gerald's incomes. Therefore, they both have to pay the same 5% of $800 ($40) in sales tax. However, since $40 is a higher percentage of the $45,000 that Gerald makes than it is of the $65,000 that Liss makes, Gerald, who earns less, is paying a higher percentage of his income in tax. Sales taxes, then, tend to hit poorer people harder than they do those with lots of money.

Finally, there are also **proportional taxes**. A proportional tax is one in which everyone pays the same amount *proportional* to their income. A proportional income tax, for example, would be one in which everyone pays a set percent (say, 10%) of their annual income. Therefore, Joe, who earns $100,000, would pay 10% ($10,000); Anne, who earns $50,000, would pay 10% ($5,000); and Beverly, who earns $25,000, would pay 10% ($2500). Although they each pay different amounts, the amounts are the same proportionally. They all pay 10%.

FISCAL POLICY AND INFLATION

Bull Market

As we studied earlier, *inflation* is a rise in prices. The government can actually use fiscal policy to encourage or help stop inflation. When taxes are high, inflation decreases. High taxes mean that people have to pay more of their income to the government. This leaves less money for spending in the marketplace. As a result, demand for products drops. Producers, then, must lower prices to encourage consumers to spend the little bit of money that they have on their products. On the other hand, when taxes are low, inflation

102

increases for the opposite reason. Now consumers can keep and spend more money. It is not as hard for producers to get consumers to spend money on their products. Therefore, they can afford to raise their prices and still do well.

THE IMPACT OF MONETARY POLICY

Monetary policy, as we have already discussed, refers to the actions taken by the Federal Reserve to control the money supply. The Fed primarily controls the flow of money by means of: 1) raising/lowering the reserve requirement, 2) raising/lowering the discount rate, and 3) open market operations (Review chapter 3 if necessary). When the Fed raises or lowers the reserve requirement, it makes it harder or easier for banks to loan money. When the Fed raises or lowers the discount rate, it results in banks charging higher or lower interest on loans. Finally, when the Fed buys or sells bonds (open market operations) it either: 1) encourages consumers to save by selling them bonds as an investment, or 2) encourages consumers to spend by buying their bonds and giving them money back with interest. Again, to see how monetary policy affects average citizens, let's look at some practical examples.

THE RESERVE REQUIREMENT

New Home

Nancy and Phil are a young couple with a one-year-old daughter. After four years of marriage, they feel ready to buy their first house. They go to the bank and apply for a loan. Fortunately, they have decent credit and Phil makes enough to qualify. They pay $10,000 down and take out a home loan for $135,000 at 5.7% interest (5.7 % of the loan amount is how much money Nancy and Phil will have to pay annually for using the bank's money to buy their house). A month later, Charlie and Rachel decide to buy a home as well. Because they don't yet have a

child, Rachel and Charlie both work. Therefore, they earn a little more income than Nancy and Phil. They also have decent credit and want to buy a house in the same neighborhood that is priced approximately the same as Nancy and Phil's. However, during the period between the time Nancy and Phil were approved for their loan and Rachel and Charlie applied for theirs, the Federal Reserve raised the reserve requirement. As you remember from chapter 3, this means that the bank must now keep more money on hand and loan less. As a result, the bank must limit the number of people that qualify for loans. Therefore, it raises the interest rate from 5.7% to 6.5%. It now cost more to borrow $135,000 than it did a month earlier. The result is that, because their interest rate was lower, Nancy and Phil made enough income to qualify for a loan. However, now, with a higher interest rate making the monthly payments higher, Charlie and Rachel do not earn enough to qualify and the bank turns them down. They will have to keep renting until either their income increases or interest rates drop. Had they applied earlier, when the reserve requirement was less and interest rates lower, they most likely would have gotten their loan. Meanwhile, there may be a third couple, Roger and Lisa, who qualify for the loan, but because of the higher payments accompanying a 6.5% interest rate, they know that they simply could not afford the monthly payments. As a result, they to have to pass on buying a house even though the bank would have given them the money. In each case, all three couples were affected by the Federal Reserve's monetary policy.

DISCOUNT RATE

Once again, when the Federal Reserve raises or lowers the discount rate, it determines how much interest banks must pay to the Fed to borrow money. The more interest banks must pay the Fed, the higher interest they must charge people to borrow. When the discount rate is high, banks tend to borrow less in order to avoid paying high interest. Therefore, they have less money to loan. The fact that they have less money also contributes to higher interest rates (remember, when demand is high and supply scarce, prices rise. In the case of financial institutions, when the supply of money is scarce and demand high, they raise interest rates).

How does this affect individuals? Well, we've already seen the affects of high interest rates on those wanting to borrow money in the examples of Rachel and Charlie and Roger and Lisa. People are able to consume less because they can't borrow as much money. There are other effects as well. Say that Samuel has $5,000. He can either use the money as a down payment on a new boat or save it. Since the Fed has recently raised the reserve requirement, interest rates are high. As a result, Samuel decides to save his $5,000 because he knows he can earn high interest,

Boats in Marina

whereas, if he used it on a down payment on a boat, he would have to pay high interest on any additional amount he borrowed. He will wait until interest rates drop before getting his boat. Sounds good, right? But what about Brandon who owns a boat dealership? Because interest rates are high, more people are saving money rather than spending it on large items like boats. As a result, Brandon sells only half of what he hoped to sell over the spring and summer. His profits are much less than he anticipated. Therefore, he cannot afford to have as many employees. He has no choice but to fire Julio and Mary Anne, and he ends up having to cut back Francine to part-time hours, thereby paying her less. Obviously, this affects Julio, Mary Anne, Francine, and their families. Conversely, if interest rates are low, Samuel and many others buy their boats, Brandon makes more money, Julio, Mary Anne, and Francine get raises, and Rafael gets a job because Brandon finds that he needs additional help.

OPEN MARKET OPERATIONS

Open market operations involves the government selling securities (bonds). When the government sells bonds, it is allowing people to save money by loaning it to the government in exchange for interest. When this happens, people are encouraged to save via bonds. This means they are buying less and, again, consumption, prices, profits, and production ultimately drop. On the other hand, when the government buys bonds, it is putting money back into the hands of bond holders as it buys their bonds back with interest. This pumps money into the economy as individuals spend more. They buy homes, cars, take vacations, go out to eat more, and buy or do all the other things they would not spend money on when they were saving. To summarize: selling bonds encourages people to save their money in bonds, while buying bonds encourages them to spend.

Suppose the Fed decides to sell securities. Mary has $10,000 on hand that she would normally spend in the economy. However, because she realizes that she can loan money to the government through bonds at a high interest rate, she elects to use the money to purchase bonds instead. All that money is now in savings rather than spent. That means that Mary is not eating at restaurants she otherwise would have, is not buying clothes from stores she otherwise would have shopped at, is not taking trips she perhaps would have booked, etc. That means less money for waiters, retail sales people, travel agents, hotels, etc. However, when the Fed buys securities back and Mary gets her $10,000 plus interest, all that money will go into the economy (assuming she doesn't just save and invest it all) and waiters, salespeople, travel agents, etc. will make more money.

Practice 5.3 Fiscal and Monetary Policy

1. Darlene would love to take a trip to Hawaii. However, when she gets her taxes back from her accountant, she realizes that she will have to pay as much to the government in taxes as it would have cost to take the trip to Hawaii. As a result, Darlene decides not to go on her trip. Darlene's financial decision making has been impacted by

    A. the government's monetary policy.
    B. the Federal Reserve's monetary policy.
    C. the government's fiscal policy.
    D. open market operations.

2. If the Federal Reserve lowers the reserve requirement, Bobby, as a consumer, will be more likely to

    A. buy a house.
    B. save his money.
    C. buy bonds.
    D. pay a high interest rate.

3. How does changing the reserve requirement and/or the discount rate impact individuals hoping to borrow money?

4. Would someone who owns a car dealership most likely prefer that the government buy bonds or sell them? Explain your answer.

5.4 CREDIT AND INSURANCE

CREDIT

Credit Cards

In today's society, people often purchase things on credit. **Credit** is an agreement under which a buyer receives goods or services at the present time in exchange for a promise to pay for them at a future time. One reason that consumers buy goods or services on credit is that their future income may be more promising than their current income. For example, college students may take out student loans because they have little current income. Once they receive their degree, however, they will start earning a substantial income with which they can pay back the borrowed funds. Consumers also buy on credit because some items are so expensive that it is difficult to save the entire lump sum before purchasing. For example, saving enough money to buy a house in one full payment is too difficult for most people. Houses simply cost too much money and, unless you're Brad Pitt or Oprah Winfrey, you probably don't have several hundred thousand dollars just sitting around waiting to be spent. Most people can, however, afford to buy a house if they can pay for it a little at a time. Therefore, just like in our example of Nancy and Phil, they usually pay a small percentage up front, then borrow the rest on credit which they pay back in monthly installments. Such a loan is called a *mortgage* and the monthly installments are referred to as *mortgage payments*. (Most mortgages are paid back over either fifteen or thirty years.)

INTEREST

Throughout this book, we have occasionally referred to the concept of *interest*. As defined in an earlier chapter, **interest** is the amount of money that a lender charges a borrower in exchange for the use of their money. When you take out a loan from a bank or credit union to buy a home, car, boat, finance an education, make home repairs, etc. you are using the bank or credit union's money to pay for these things in exchange for monthly payments with interest. When you take out a school loan, you are using the money of whichever lender provided you with the finances to go to school in

Using Credit Card

exchange for paying it back after you graduate with interest. One of the most popular ways people purchase things today is with **credit cards**. Credit cards are popular because they are very convenient and allow people to pay for things without having to write checks, constantly keep up with how much money is left in their checking account, and/or carry around lots of cash. Consumers often purchase whatever items they can on a credit card and then pay them off with one payment. Again, however, when you use a credit card you have to pay interest. Why? Because you are using the company's money that issued you the card to make a purchase in exchange for paying for the item later. We should mention that *debit cards* and credit cards are not the same. When you use a credit card, you are borrowing the credit card issuers money as a loan that you will pay back with interest. However, when you use a debit card, you are simply using something that looks like a credit card to access your own money (usually in a checking account). Therefore, debit purchases are the same as spending cash or writing a check. It's your own money, so you pay no interest. When using debit cards, however, it is important to keep up with how much you are spending because, once the money in your account is used up, there will be nothing left to access.

Debt

In summary then, the advantage of credit is that it allows consumers to pay for items and obtain goods that they otherwise could not afford. Credit allows people to pay for things later or over time. The disadvantage, however, is that borrowers have to pay interest in addition to the cost of the good. This means that the good actually ends up costing the consumer much more money than it would have had they simply paid for it up front. Sadly, because credit cards can be used so easily, many consumers borrower more than they can afford to pay back. As a result, they end up fighting to get out of debt, only to find that the interest they are charged accumulates faster than they can pay back their loan. Some even go bankrupt! It is important that consumers use credit cards wisely and only to make purchases they can afford to pay back in a relatively short amount of time. Otherwise, they run the risk of getting into too much debt and suffering terrible financial consequences.

SIMPLE AND COMPOUND INTEREST

Interest is based on a percentage of the total amount of money loaned. As a consumer, it is important to understand how interest rates work. There are essentially two types of interest, *simple* and *compound*. When deciding whether or not to borrow money, you need to know which type of interest you will be paying on the loan! **Simple interest** is a rate that is applied only to the value of the *principal*. The **principal** is the amount of money that has been borrowed. For example, say Jeff takes out a ten-year loan at a rate of 5% annually on $10,000 in principal. In other words, he borrows $10,000 and agrees to pay it back a little at a time over a ten-year period. Because he will pay 5% annual interest only on the $10,000 principal, Jeff will be paying *simple interest*. The total interest he has to pay will be 5% of 10,000 for every year he is paying on the loan. Therefore, Jeff's total payment after ten years would be $15,000:

$10,000 for the loan amount + {5% of 10,000 ($500) X 10 (because it is a ten year pay period)}

Since $500 X 10 = $5,000, the total amount Jeff pays would be $10,000 + $5,000 = $15,000.

Compound interest, however, is much different. It is interest applied to both the principal and the *accrued interest*. In other words, the borrower does not simply pay a percentage of the original loan amount. Instead, they must pay interest on the amount including the additional interest as it builds over time. Let's consider the example of Jeff's $10,000 loan again, only this time, let's say that Jeff has to pay the loan back at *compound* rather than *simple interest*. We can determine the value of the compound interest using the following formula:

$$A = P \times \left[1 + \frac{r}{n} \right]^{nt}$$

A= the total value to be repaid ; P= Principal ($10,000); r= interest rate (5%)

n= the number of compounding periods per year (in Jeff's case, it only compounds once/year) = 1

t= number of years of the loan = 10

Applying the formula above, we now see that Jeff will pay $6,288.95 in interest rather than $5,000. We get this amount by taking the total value repaid ($16,288.95) and subtracting the original amount of the loan ($10,000). Since 6,288.95 is the amount left over, we know that this is the amount paid in interest.

In some cases, the number of times interest compounds may change. For instance, some loans may compound every six months (n=2) or every month (n=12). If the number of compounding periods per year changes, the value of interest paid changes as well. As you can see, compounding interest can drastically increase the value to be repaid. Compound interest is a bad thing if you are borrowing money, because it increases the amount that you have to pay back. On the other hand, it is a good thing when you are saving and investing money, because it means that your money is growing at a much faster rate than if you were receiving only simple interest.

In general, the higher the risk to the lender, the higher the interest rate. In other words, the greater the chance that the lender will not be paid back and that it will not be able to get back the value of the loan, the more interest it will charge. Home loans, therefore, tend to have lower interest rates than credit cards or auto loans. Homes can't be easily stolen and it is easy to find the borrower because they are living in the home itself. Also, because it is such a big purchase, borrowers normally meet stricter requirements than they do for certain other types of loans. If the borrower *defaults* (fails to pay back the loan), then the lender can repossess the house and sell it to cover at least part of its losses. Items bought using credit cards, however, are riskier. Many citizens get so deep in credit card debt that they can't pay all the money back. Also, many of the items purchased cannot be repossessed (i.e., meals, education, various services, products that are old or no longer good, trips taken, etc.). As a result, interest rates on credit cards are usually much higher than on most other types of loans.

CREDIT WORTHINESS

Debt is the amount of money that you owe on money that you have borrowed. Too much debt can cause people to default on loans (fail to pay them back). When people can't pay back the money they've borrowed to buy cars, boats, furniture, etc. these items are often re-possessed (taken) by the lender. Failure to pay your debts also damages your **credit score**. Your credit score is a number based on your history as a borrower. If you have a history of paying off loans and making monthly credit payments on time, then you will have a high credit score. If, however, you

Credit Report

are normally late with payments or have defaulted on loans, you will have a low credit score. Lenders use your credit score to determine your **credit worthiness**. In other words, they look at your credit score to determine what the chances are that you will pay back the loan. How much of a risk lenders think you are will go a long way in deciding whether or not they loan you money and/or what interest rate they will charge you. If you have a high credit score, then lenders are more likely to loan you money at a lower interest rate. However, if you have a low credit score, then your interest rate will be higher because you are considered to be a greater risk for the lender. Often, if your score is low enough, you won't get a loan at all. As you can see, it is very important that citizens prove trustworthy and pay back any money they owe on time. Otherwise, they run the risk of not being able to borrow in the future.

In addition to your credit history, other factors are important as well. For instance, how much money do you make and/or have in savings? How much property do you own? The higher your income and the more money you have in savings, investments, etc., the less risk you pose to a lender. The more money you have, the more confident lenders are that you will pay back the loan. Similarly, the more property you own, the more collateral you have to insure the loan.

Finally, how many debts you currently have can also determine your credit worthiness. Even if you have a history of paying debts on time, if a lender sees that you already have several thousand dollars in credit card debts, a large house payment, school loan payments, and a number of other lenders you owe money to, they will be less likely to grant you a loan. Why? The more people you owe money to, the more money you are paying to lenders. The more you are paying lenders, the less you have left over to make payments on any new money you might borrow.

INSURANCE

Dealing with Disability

Insurance involves transferring risk to others. An individual or household has something of great value and wants to make sure that, if it is lost or damaged, it will be financially covered. For this reason, they invest in **insurance**. They pay money to an insurance company (usually monthly) for the assurance that, if what they value is lost or damaged, the insurance company will pay for their loss (either in full or in part). Insurance is especially popular when it comes to things that households or businesses would likely not have the funds to pay for on their own. **Life insurance** is meant to provide money to one's family if they die. Say Martin provides the main income for his family of six. If Martin didn't work, his family could not pay their mortgage, car payment, etc. What happens if Martin dies? How will Martin's family make it? To make sure they would be OK, Martin buys life insurance. Martin pays money monthly to the insurance company which, if he dies, will provide his family with the money they need to live. Martin may either buy term life insurance, which simply pays money to his beneficiary (the person Martin wants the money to go to); or he may buy what is often called whole life insurance, which is generally more expensive and builds cash value like an investment. There are other types of insurance as well. **Health/medical insurance** is meant to cover health and medical expenses, many of which can be outrageously expensive. **Disability insurance** provides a policy-holder with income in the event that they become disabled and unable to work. For instance, say a factory worker is hurt in a fall and cannot stand on the assembly line, or an office worker is injured in a car wreck and can't come to work for two months. Disability insurance provides up to 60% of their income until they can work again and receive their normal paycheck. (Note that disability will not pay a disabled worker 100% of their income because the law forbids it. If workers received 100% of their normal income through disability insurance, then there would be no incentive to return to work. People could make as much staying at home, pretending to still be disabled.)

Car Wreck

A broad category of insurance is **liability insurance**. Liability insurance pays if you are held financially liable (responsible) for an accident. For instance, automobile liability insurance pays for damages someone caused with their automobile (i.e., causing a wreck).

Homeowner insurance

Hospital Patient

policies, which cover a policy holders house in the event it is damaged or destroyed, often include liability as well. If someone falls in your yard and then successfully sues you to pay for their injuries, then your liability insurance will pay the cost. In general, then, liability insurance provides protection from claims arising from injuries or damage to other people or property. **Comprehensive liability** insurance covers a much wider range of catastrophes. Businesses need comprehensive liability to cover injuries that occur on business property, accidents due to employee negligence, property damage caused by company workers, losses or injuries caused by defective products, and any professional mistakes (i.e., medical malpractice on the part of a doctor). In short, the benefit of insurance is that it protects the policy-holder and/or their beneficiaries from financial devastation in the event that a major catastrophe occurs. However, the cost is that it requires people and businesses to pay money for insurance that could otherwise be saved, invested, or used for consumption. It also is money that may never be used (i.e., no disability ever occurs).

Practice 5.4   Credit and Insurance

1. An agreement in which a buyer receives goods or services at the present time in exchange for a promise to pay for them at a later time is called

    A. debt.   B.   interest.   C.   interest rate.   D.   credit.

2. Which of the following people would benefit the most from compound interest?
    A.   someone applying for a home loan.
    B.   someone who needs a car loan.
    C.   someone investing their money in an IRA.
    D.   a borrower with a high credit score.

3. Describe the difference between simple and compound interest. Why would a borrower or investor want to know ahead of time what kind of interest is going to be added to their loan/investment?

4. What is the purpose of insurance?

CHAPTER 5 REVIEW

Key terms and concepts

positive incentive	the impact of monetary policy
negative incentive	debt
rational decision making model	credit
commercial banks	interest
interest charged	credit cards
interest earned	simple interest
credit unions	principal
savings and loan associations	compound interest
return	credit score
risk	credit worthiness
stocks	insurance
mutual funds	
bonds	
retirement	
workers' earnings	
the impact of fiscal policy	

Multiple Choice Questions:

1. Gary wants to save for retirement. However, he is no expert in investing and needs someone who knows more than him helping him handle his money wisely. Gary doesn't desire to get rich quick; he just wants to know that his money is growing over the next thirty years until he is 65. Since Gary's top priority seems to be steady growth and security for his money, the BEST option for him would be what?

    A. to put all of his savings in the stock of whatever company is currently performing the best on the New York Stock Exchange

    B. to put all of his money in a relatively unknown stock that is likely to do well

    C. to invest in a mutual fund

    D. to purchase collateral

2. Miriam's boss has expressed his displeasure with Miriam's job performance recently at work. He tells her that if she does not get her department in order, she will soon be demoted from her current position. Miriam's boss is attempting to motivate her with

    A. a low rate of interest.

    B. a negative incentive.

    C. a rational decision making process.

    D. a set principle.

3. Having a college degree often results in

    A. higher worker earnings.

    B. compound interest.

    C. a lower discount rate.

    D. a lower credit score.

4. Barbara and Chad are starting their own small business. However, because their funds are limited, they will need a loan from the bank to purchase some of the equipment they need. They will also have to charge a number of items to their new business credit card. Barbara and Chad are purchasing all these items

   A.   for less than the principal.   C.   on credit.

   B.   in hopes that interest rates are high.   D.   as lenders.

5. George deposits $100, 000 in Kennesaw Mountain Bank. A year later, he borrows $100,000 from Kennesaw Mountain Bank to finance his son's college education. Which of the following statements is true?

   A.   George did not have to prove he had collateral.

   B.   George is being paid compound interest by the bank.

   C.   George is being charged more interest than he's earning.

   D.   George is earning more interest than he's charged.

6. The government's fiscal policy affects private citizens because it

   A.   determines how high interest rates are.

   B.   determines how much money they have available to spend.

   C.   lowers their credit scores.

   D.   makes it harder for them to qualify for insurance.

7. Tito owns a restaurant in midtown Atlanta. Tito would probably like it if

   A.   the Fed would raise the reserve requirement.   C.   Congress would raise taxes.

                                         D.   there was a higher discount rate.

   B.   the Fed would buy bonds.

8. Brenda and Kyle have identical credit histories. They each take out a $20,000 loan at 6% interest over 12 years from the same lender. However, at the end of 12 years, Brenda has paid the lender roughly $40,000, while Kyle has only paid $34,400. The reason for the difference is most likely because

   A.   Brenda and Kyle each had different principals.

   B.   Brenda had a lower credit score than Kyle.

   C.   Brenda's loan paid compound interest while Kyle's paid simple interest.

   D.   the lender discriminates against women.

9. Your credit worthiness is determined LEAST by which of the following?

   A.   credit score   B.   collateral   C.   amount of debt   D.   tax rate

Georgia US Economics
Practice Test 1

The purpose of this practice test is to measure your progress in US economics. This test is based on the GPS-based EOCT standards for US economics and adheres to the sample question format provided by the Georgia Department of Education.

General Directions:

1. Read all directions carefully.

2. Read each question or sample. Then choose the best answer.

3. Choose only one answer for each question. If you change an answer, be sure to erase your original answer completely.

1   Doctor Baskin is a dentist, but, as F1 a hobby, he restores vintage cars and enters them in auto shows. Currently, Baskin works at his practice five days a week and forty-eight weeks a year. Seeing about twenty patients a day, at an average of $50 per patient, the doctor's practice makes about $5,000 a week, or $240,000 per year. However, Baskin, who loves his hobby dearly, is considering going to a four day work week forty-five weeks a year. This will allow him to spend every Friday working on cars, and will give him three weeks to prepare for the big shows. Baskin figures that he can go from making $500 per year to $2,500 a year in prize money at the car shows. Baskin decides to proceed with the four day week, what is his opportunity cost?

A   The decision to change schedules is the opportunity cost.

B   The opportunity cost is the $2,000 increase in prizes and the time spent working on cars.

C   The opportunity cost is about $58,000 per year (i.e. $60,000 less dentistry income minus the additional prize income).

D   The opportunity cost is the reduced time spent working on teeth and the increased time he will be forced to work on cars.

2   The market for labor would be MI1 considered a _____ market.

A   product
B   factor
C   wage
D   monopolistic

3   Which of the following state- PF2 ments BEST describes the operation of banks?

A   Banks take in deposits, for which they pay a relatively small rate of interest, they then hold a small amount aside and loan out the rest at a higher rate of interest.

B   Banks borrow money from the government at low interest rates and they loan that money to customers at higher interest rates.

C   Banks, under license from the government, print money that they then loan out to businesses and households.

D   Banks take in deposits which they use to pay their employees and other costs.

4   What effect does a "tight MA2 money" policy have on the reserve requirement and the economy's money supply?

A   It raises the reserve requirement, thereby increasing the money supply.

B   It lowers the reserve requirement, thereby decreasing the money supply.

C   It raises the reserve requirement, thereby decreasing the money supply.

D   It lowers the reserve requirement, thereby increasing the money supply.

5   Which of the following economic IN1 systems is BEST at providing incentives to produce?

A   traditional
B   command
C   market
D   mercantilist

6 Below is a schedule that shows the number of pairs of socks that producers MI2 are willing to make and that consumers are willing to purchase at various prices. In a perfect market economy, for what price will the socks be sold?

Price	Produced	Demanded
$0.50	0	1,000
$1.00	100	900
$1.50	200	800
$2.00	300	700
$2.50	400	600
$3.00	500	500
$3.50	600	400
$4.00	700	300
$4.50	800	200
$5.00	900	100
$5.50	1,000	0

A $1.50   **B** $2.00   **C** $3.00   **D** $4.50

7 Using the table from the previ- MI3 ous question, what would happen if the price for socks was set at $2.50 per pair?

A market clearance

B a shortage

C a surplus

D no socks would be produced

8 Floating exchange rates are IN3 determined by

A supply and demand.

B the president of the US.

C the central bank.

D the stock of gold reserves.

9 A recession is a MA1

A period of declining government spending.

B period of increasing government spending.

C period of increasing taxation.

D period of declining national income.

10 Congresswoman Jenkins, a rep- EF5 resentative for the state of California, is concerned about the plight of the aerospace industry. She is afraid that jet manufacturers will go out of business because profits are too low. This would mean a loss of jobs for many of her constituents. As a solution, Jenkins proposes a price floor. What would be the LIKELY result of such an action?

A a shortage of planes

B The problem will be solved without adverse effects.

C an increase in the quality of the planes

D a surplus of planes

GO ON

11 Taiwanese baseballs now sell in   IN2 the US for $10, but a domestically made baseball of identical quality sells for $12.50. If the US government were to impose a 20% tariff on Taiwanese baseballs, what would be the result?

A   Since the Taiwanese ball would still be cheaper than the US ball, there may not be much change in the sales of Taiwanese baseballs.

B   Since the Taiwanese ball is now more expensive than the US ball, US sales will likely increase.

C   Since the Taiwanese ball will now sell at the same price as the US ball, sales will likely equalize.

D   Since the Taiwanese ball is now more expensive, the US will begin exporting baseballs to Taiwan.

12 A flat tax is one that takes a   PF3 fixed percentage of every tax payers income. Which type of tax would BEST describe such a tax?

A   proportional
B   progressive
C   regressive
D   invasive

13 The United States economy is   EF3 one in which producers are generally free to produce what they want and consumers are free to purchase what they desire, so long as no laws are broken. At the same time, however, the government does regulate some aspects of the economy. The US can BEST be described as which of the following.

A   a market economy
B   command economy
C   liberated economy
D   mixed economy

14 The table below gives the number   IN1 of motorcycles and fish produced by 100 workers in a week for the countries of Germany and Greece. Assume these countries do not currently engage in trade in these products. Which of the following statements BEST describes the situation?

	Motorcycles	Fish
Germany	500	10
Greece	5	100

A   Germany has an absolute advantage in both products, but Greece should still specialize in fish.

B   Germany has an absolute advantage in motorcycles, and Greece has an absolute advantage in fish.

C   Germany has a comparative advantage is motorcycles, but Greece has an absolute advantage in both products.

D   In this particular case, neither side would benefit from specializing more in one of the particular products.

15 Consumers reduce spending   MA1 because they lack confidence in the economy and their prospects for future employment. All else being equal, what effect will this have on the price level and real GDP?

A   Both prices and real GDP will decline.

B   Both prices and real GDP will increase.

C   Prices will increase, but real GDP will be unaffected because aggregate demand only influences nominal GDP.

D   Prices will decrease, but real GDP will be unaffected because aggregate demand only influences nominal GDP.

Use the graph below to answer question 16.

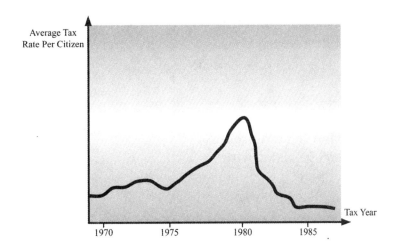

16 In what year would consumers have been MOST LIKELY to spend more   PF3
money in the marketplace?

  A   1974   B   1977   C   1980   D   1984

17 Which of the following BEST   PF6
explains why mechanical engineers are paid more than janitors?

  A   engineers make more money for a
       firm and are in shorter supply

  B   engineers are more educated than
       janitors

  C   engineers do mental work but jani-
       tors do physical work

  D   engineers work longer hours than
       janitors

18 Belinda has a business making   EF1
steel ornamental lawn statues.
The machine she uses to join pieces of
steel together is considered

  A   human capital.

  B   entrepreneurship.

  C   labor.

  D   capital.

19 Phil has great healthcare cover-   PF5
age through his job. However,
Phil has to pay $125 out of every pay-
check in order to help cover the cost
of the company's health care plan.
The good part is that the $125 is tax
free. Phil's monthly payment to help
cover health care can BEST be
described as

  A   a benefit of insurance.

  B   a cost of insurance.

  C   a fiscal policy.

  D   an opportunity cost.

20 Which of the following is an   PF1
important reason why people
need financial investment plans?

  A   to know where to purchase goods

  B   to save for retirement

  C   to gain simple rather than com-
       pound interest

  D   to lower their credit score

GO ON

21 Which of the following are responsible for making fiscal policy decisions?   MA3

    A   the president and Congress

    B   the Federal Reserve System

    C   the National Council of Economic Advisor

    D   the Commerce Department

22 Which of the following is a problem MOST often associated with command economies?   EF4

    A   Public goods are underproduced.

    B   The goods that consumers want are often undersupplied while those consumers don't want are sometimes oversupplied.

    C   There is a huge income disparity between the richest and poorest citizens.

    D   high unemployment rates

23 Amy is excited because she just opened her own consulting firm. Amy loves being her own boss and not having to consult with anyone else before she makes decisions. Eventually, she even hopes to incorporate and enjoy some additional tax advantages. The only downside is that she has invested all the money herself. If the business fails, she could go bankrupt. What kind of business does Amy own?   MI4

    A   sole proprietorship

    B   partnership

    C   cooperative

    D   corporation

24 Which of the following statements BEST describes the concept of the business cycle?   MA1

    A   the flow of money from businesses to households as income

    B   the flow of goods from businesses to households and labor from households to businesses

    C   the flow of funds from product markets to factor market and the flow of resources from factor markets to product markets

    D   alternating periods of economic growth and decline

25 Lola is selling *Happy Teen* magazine at her school to raise money for a trip to Washington, DC. The marginal cost of each magazine she buys is $2.00, and the price she sells them for is $5.00. Yesterday, she got a letter in the mail saying that the magazine was raising its cost per magazine from $2.00 to $3.50. Today, Mrs. Ibarra pulls Lola aside and informs her that, from now on, she will only be allowed to sell the magazine for $3.25 at school. What has happened to Lola's incentive to produce?   MI2

    A   She will have less incentive to produce because the higher marginal cost lowers her profits.

    B   She will have more incentive to produce because she will sell more at the lower prices and make more profits.

    C   Her incentive to produce will remain unchanged because she still wants to go to Washington, DC.

    D   She will have no incentive to produce because with the change in marginal cost and price, she will no longer make a profit.

26 Bill must decide between using EF2 the $20 he has on hand to either go to the movies with his best friend, Nate, or buy a gift for the girl he likes, Sarah. If Bill decides that the marginal benefit he would get from buying Sarah the gift is greater than the marginal cost, the rational economic choice for Bill would be

A   to go to the movies with Nate.

B   to buy Sarah a gift.

C   to avoid any opportunity cost.

D   to save his resources for another time.

27 Phil Hassan is a farmer. Phil is MI2 selling two parcels of land that are each 40 acres in area. Parcel A sells for $25,000 and parcel B sells for $55,000. Which of the following would BEST explain the difference in price between the two parcels?

A   There is a greater supply of parcel A land than parcel B land.

B   There is a greater supply of parcel B land than parcel A land.

C   There is a greater demand for parcel A land than parcel B land.

D   There is a greater demand for parcel B land than parcel A land.

28 The Panamanian balboa (currency) always exchanges at a IN3 rate of one balboa = 1 US dollar. The balboa has a(n)—

A   floating exchange rate.

B   appreciating exchange rate.

C   depreciating exchange rate.

D   fixed exchange rate.

29 Throughout the 1990s, the government of the country of Lydia MA1 spent much more than it received in taxes. Because of this, Lydia owed $100 billion in 2002. However, for the past two years, Lydia has taken in $5 billion more in taxes per year than it spent. Which of the following can accurately be said of Lydia?

A   Lydia ran budget surpluses in the 1990s, but now it is out of debt.

B   Lydia is now experiencing budget surpluses, but it is still in debt.

C   Lydia ran budget deficits in the 1990s, but is now out of debt.

D   Lydia is now experiencing budget deficits, and is still in debt.

30 Which of the following statements is true regarding house- MI1 holds, businesses, and government in the US economic system?

A   Households pay taxes to the government, but businesses don't.

B   Households act as consumers while government and businesses act only as producers.

C   The three are economically interdependent on one another.

D   Government regulates what businesses can produce, but not what consumers can buy.

31 In a market economy, what is the MI3 primary motivation for producers to sell their products at a price consumers can afford?

A   patriotism

B   sense of duty

C   profit

D   fear of government regulations

GO ON

32 Which of the following is an
    assumption of command
    economies? EF4

    A The means of production will be
       privately owned.

    B Transactions will be voluntary on
       both the part of the buyer and the
       seller.

    C The government's economic role
       will be minimal.

    D Wealth and resources will be equi-
       tably distributed.

33 This table shows quarterly GDP
    for the US between 2001 and
    2003. Between which two quarters
    was there a decline in productivity? MA1

Year-Quarter	Real GDP
2001-I	100.597
2001-II	100.906
2001-III	100.551
2001-IV	100.948
2002-I	101.798
2002-II	102.400
2002-III	103.059
2002-IV	103.249
2003-I	103.743
2003-II	104.792
2003-III	106.681
2003-IV	107.780

    A between the first and second
       quarter of 2001

    B between the second and third quar-
       ter of 2001

    C between the third and fourth quar-
       ter of 2002

    D between the fourth quarter of 2002
       and the first quarter of 2003

34 Which of the following is consid-
    ered a negative side-effect of a
    minimum wage? EF1

    A full employment

    B increased interest rates

    C unemployment

    D failure to meet equilibrium pro-
       duction

35 In a market economy, if there is
    not a price at which both pro-
    ducers are willing to make an item
    and consumers are willing to buy the
    item, then MI2

    A it will not be made.

    B the seller will always cut their
       price.

    C the buyer will always accept a
       higher price.

    D the government will subsidize the
       product.

36 Which of the following would
    consumers MOST OFTEN need
    to consider when trying to make a
    rational economic decision? EF2

    A the impact of government
       subsidies

    B potential opportunity costs

    C factors of production

    D net exports

37 In market capitalism, which of
    the following concepts creates
    the incentive to produce? EF4

    A profits

    B low prices

    C equal distribution of resources

    D charity

38 To stimulate the economy, the
    Federal Reserve decides that the
    amount of money in circulation needs
    to increase. Which of the following
    actions will they be MOST LIKELY
    to take? MA2

    A Raise the reserve requirement.

    B Raise the discount rate.

    C Sell bonds.

    D Lower the reserve requirement.

39 Which of the following statements MOST ACCURATELY defines the term "interest rate"?   PF4

A   the level of attention that economists pay to economic activity at any one time

B   money paid by banks and financial institutions to the US government

C   money paid by a borrower to a lender in exchange for the use of money

D   discounts on purchases made with a credit card

40 Brian wants to get a promotion at work. Which of the following is a step Brian can take to help him achieve his goal?   PF6

A   Increase his number of capital investments.

B   Pay more subsidies.

C   Better assess his opportunity costs.

D   Invest in additional training.

41 Which of the following would be considered human capital?   EF6

A   a milling machine run by a machinist

B   a computer-assisted drawing software program operated by an architect

C   a training course taken by employees of a manufacturing firm

D   an assembly line for producing boats

42 In an effort to bring down the government of Fidel Castro, the United States adopted a policy of refusing to trade with Cuba. More than 40 years later, this policy remains in effect. Which of the following is an attempt to punish another country by refusing to trade with it?   IN2

A   a tariff

B   a negative trade balance

C   an embargo

D.   a trade treaty

43 Amanda is offered a raise and a brand new office if she can double her sales totals of the previous year. Amanda's employers are attempting to motivate her with   PF1

A   a negative incentive.

B   compound interest.

C   a positive incentive.

D   human capital.

44 The country of Tilio exports 20% more than it imports on average each year. By comparison, the nation of Maximo imports 10% more than it exports. Which of the following statements is true?   IN1

A   Tilio has a better exchange rate than Maximo.

B   Tilio enjoys a favorable balance of trade, while Maximo experiences an unfavorable balance of trade.

C   Tilio has an unfavorable balance of trade while Maximo's is favorable.

D   Tilio's exchange rate is less favorable than Maximo's.

Practice Test 1   Session II   Do not begin until your teacher tells you to.

Imports and Exports for Select Countries

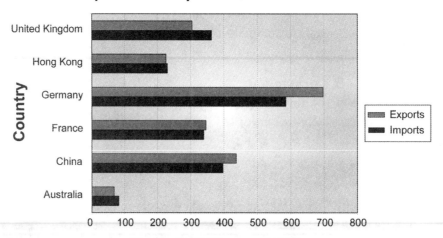

Trade in Billions of US$

45 According to the graph, which countries are experiencing a trade deficit?   IN3

A   Australia, Hong Kong, and the United Kingdom

B   Australia, Hong Kong, and France

C   France, Germany, and China

D   Germany, China, and the United Kingdom

46 Cecilia owns a coffee shop herself, but her shop is part of a national chain which supplies her with products, trains her employees, and gives her name-brand recognition. In return, she pays the chain a fee and agrees to abide by certain rules and guidelines. What type of business does Cecilia own?   MI4

A   cooperative

B   sole proprietorship

C   partnership

D   franchise

47 If one wanted to know whether there had been inflation or not, the BEST measure to observe would be the   MA1

A   GDP.

B   business cycle.

C   CPI

D   national debt

48 Someone concerned that they could not afford to pay their medical bills if they were ever in a serious accident should definitely consider investing in   PF5

   A   health bonds.

   B   stocks that are likely to perform well.

   C   insurance.

   D   workout equipment.

49 If the income of consumers declines, what will be the MOST LIKELY effect on the equilibrium price and quantity of candy?   MI1

   A   Both price and quantity will decline.

   B   Both price and quantity will rise.

   C   Prices will rise but quantity will decline.

   D   Prices will decline but quantity will rise.

50 The idea that producers will produce whatever there is sufficient demand for, as long as they can continue to make a sufficient profit, is referred to as what?   MI2

   A   supply

   B   the law of supply and demand

   C   economic equilibrium

   D   the theory of free enterprise exchange

51 If the Federal Reserve decides to sell bonds, what effect will it have?   MA2

   A   It will cause the money supply to decrease and inflation to fall.

   B   It will cause the money supply to increase and employment to rise.

   C   It will guarantee higher taxes.

   D   It will extend stagflation.

52 What is the central problem with which the study of economics is concerned?   EF1

   A   scarcity

   B   excess

   C   inflation

   D   monetary policy

53 John borrows $100 dollars from Ed. They agree that John will pay back the loan in two months at a rate of 10% monthly. If John pays back exactly $120, then the interest was   PF4

   A   compounded.

   B   simple.

   C   usurious.

   D   impounded.

54 The purpose of a tariff, when used for protectionism, is to   IN2

   A   limit the number of foreign goods imported into the country.

   B   make an imported good more expensive than its domestically produced counterpart.

   C   raise revenues to pay subsidies to domestic producers.

   D   stall importation while perishable items rot.

55 An industry that is dominated by a few large firms is   MI4

   A   monopolistic.

   B   monopolistically competitive.

   C   oligopolistic.

   D   perfectly competitive.

GO ON

56 A recession causes the bat manu- MA1
facturer Louisville Slugger to lay
off 120 employees. What type of
unemployment would this example
BEST be described as?

A   cyclical

B   frictional

C   structural

D   seasonal

57 The capital account includes IN1

A   the value of trade in goods
and services.

B   the value of foreign aid.

C   the value of trade of machines and
equipment.

D   the value of investments into and
out of the country.

58 An exchange rate which is par- IN3
tially determined by supply and
demand, but for which the central
bank may intervene if the value goes
above or below a predetermined
range of acceptable rates is called a

A   fixed exchange rate.

B   floating exchange rate.

C   managed floating exchange rate.

D   flying drift exchange rate.

59 Which of the following charac- EF4
teristics BEST defines a com-
mand economy?

A.   inequity of income distribution

B.   government ownership of the
means of production

C.   private ownership of the means of
production

D.   decentralization of economic decision making

60 The study of how firms, nations, EF1
and individuals can BEST allo-
cate their limited resources is called
what?

A   circular economic activity

B   economics

C   factoring production

D   supply and demand analysis

61 A good that is used in place of MI2
another good to meet the same
need is called what?

A   complementary good

B   capital good

C   substitute good

D   consumer good

62 Which of the following is a likely IN3
result of a depreciation of the
Japanese yen (currency) against
other currencies?

A   Japan will export more goods.

B   Japan will import more goods.

C   Japan will increase protectionism.

D   Japan will experience an embargo.

63 Which of the following would be MA1
MOST LIKELY to increase
aggregate demand?

A   increasing consumer confidence

B   declining consumer confidence

C   decreasing government spending

D   increasing the discount rate

64 A minimum wage tends to EF4
directly affect

A   a nation's trade balance.

B   fiscal policy.

C   employment rates.

D   capital gains.

65 Every year when Bonnie goes to the mountains, she stops off at her favorite country store to buy one of their awesome apple pies. Although she could buy an apple pie at the grocery store for a third of the price, she insists that no other pie compares. She willingly pays the extra money. Many others feel the same way and thus, the country store can continually sell pies charging more than the average market price. The store's price is largely due to what? MI3

- A the market equilibrium price for apple pies
- B change in quantity demanded
- C price controls
- D economic impact of consumer taste

66 This year, when Bonnie arrives at the country store mentioned in question 65, she discovers that the pies cost $1 more than they did the previous year. Bonnie is noticing what? MA1

- A a price ceiling
- B a price floor
- C inflation
- D stagflation

67 Which of the following is usually an effect of an embargo? IN2

- A Prices fall because consumers have more options.
- B Prices rise because consumers have fewer options.
- C Countries benefit because open trade is encouraged.
- D Smaller countries give in to the demands of larger countries.

" I love owning my own business; I just wish I had more freedom to do my own thing. I'm grateful for the support the corporate office provides, but I wish I could decide for myself what kind of food we serve and what kind of atmosphere to provide."

68 The above quote is MOST LIKELY from which of the following? MI4

- A a partner in a cooperative
- B owner of a franchise
- C stockholder at odds with management
- D owner of a sole proprietorship

Look at the table below and answer the following question.

69 How should boxes X and Y be labeled in the diagram above? MA2

- A X = the president, Y = congressional districts
- B X = board of governors, Y = Federal Reserve Banks
- C X = Federal Reserve President, Y = credit unions
- D X = board of governors, Y = Federal Reserve chairpersons

GO ON

70 Roger owns a house worth $200,000. Carlton owns a house worth $150,000. They both live in the same county and receive tax bills from the same tax office. Roger learns that he will have to pay $2000 in taxes for the year, while Carlton learns that he will have to pay $1500 in taxes. It appears that property taxes on homes in Carlton and Roger's county are a   PF3

   A   progressive tax.

   B   regressive tax.

   C   proportional tax.

   D   retroactive tax.

71 Trade-offs, opportunity costs, marginal benefits, marginal costs, and personal priorities are all important to consider when   EF2

   A   dealing with fiscal policy.

   B   using credit.

   C   making rational economic choices.

   D   responding to monetary policy.

72 When producers freely choose what to produce and sell without the intervention of government and consumers freely choose what they will buy and what they are willing to pay for goods and services, it is known as   EF3

   A   voluntary exchange.

   B   market analysis.

   C   command economic interaction.

   D   production possibilities.

73 Darren owns his own plumbing business. He spends some of his company's profits on new pipes and tools. Jennifer then hires Darren and his assistant to install a new septic tank in her back yard. Which of the following statements is true?   MI1

   A   Darren is labor and Jennifer is the entrepreneur.

   B   Darren is the entrepreneur, Jennifer's yard is the land, and Darren's assistant represents capital.

   C   Darren bought his tools in a factor/resource market and Jennifer paid for his services in a product market.

   D   Darren's company represents a household.

74 Mark's company produces lawn mowers. In order to increase production and profits, Mark invests thousands of dollars in a new machine that assembles lawn mower engines much more efficiently than any previous system his company has used. The machine which Mark has purchased is what?   EF6

   A   an example of improved training

   B   an example of diminishing returns

   C   an example of input over output

   D   an example of a capital good

75 Taylor is thinking of leaving the big corporation he works for and starting his own firm. He comes to you for advice and asks you what you think. As a friend, you might want to warn Taylor that starting his own firm will mean that he has   MI4

   A   no risks.

   B   to be prepared to sell stock in his company.

   C   unlimited liability.

   D   no way to get a loan.

Use the graph below to answer question number 76.

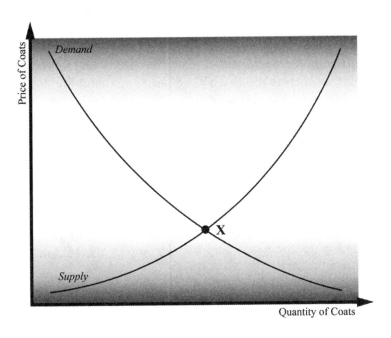

76 If the supply of coats drops below point X, then demand will   MI2
   A   automatically decline as well.
   B   exceed supply.
   C   reach equilibrium.
   D   cause a surplus.

77 Saving resources that could be   PF1
   used for immediate benefit for
   some greater benefit at a later time is
   called what?
   A   productivity
   B   investment
   C   capital good
   D   diminishing returns

78 Which of the following is NOT   EF4
   an element of the US free enter-
   prise system?
   A   voluntary exchange
   B   freedom
   C   full employment
   D   motivation to make profits

GO ON

79 David decides to start his own business. He opens a shop that manufactures sports equipment. He pays Frank an hourly wage to make baseball bats and Gene a salary to manage his finances. Three days after his grand opening, he is ecstatic because Mike, who runs the town's parks and recreation department, calls him and orders equipment for 6 little league baseball teams. Which of the following statements is true? *EF1*

   A   David is a producer, Frank is labor, Gene is the entrepreneur of the business, and Mike has just ordered capital goods.

   B   David is a producer, Frank and Gene are consumers, and Mike has just made an investment.

   C   David is the entrepreneur, Frank and Gene are both labor, and Mike is a consumer.

   D   Frank and Gene are both entrepreneurs, David is the owner, and Mike has just made a capital investment.

80 Dana's company has produced a large number of pink, rubber shoes. However, the demand for pink, rubber shoes in the marketplace is drastically less than the current supply. Which of the following situations does Dana find herself in? *MI2*

   A   She needs to raise prices to make up the difference between supply and demand.

   B   She needs to cut prices because she is experiencing a surplus.

   C   She needs to cut prices because she is experiencing a shortage.

   D   She needs to raise prices because she is experiencing a surplus.

81 Which of the following would LEAST affect the overall US economy? *MA1*

   A   Terrorists successfully blow up a major US oil pipeline and several major US oil refineries.

   B   The Supreme Court upholds a ruling that a huge corporation has established an illegal monopoly in a revolutionary new technology market and must be broken up.

   C   Several airline pilots resign because they are tired of working in an unstable industry.

   D   The president signs a bill lowering tariffs, thereby making it easier for products from other countries to be sold in the US.

82 Williams Skateboard Company decides to raise the price of skateboards by 20% because sales have been good and demand for their product very high. However, soon after the price increase, Williams Skateboard Company notices that sales quickly drop by close to 70%. Executives at Williams Skateboard underestimated what when they decided to raise prices? *MI3*

   A   the available supply of skateboards

   B   the price elasticity of their product

   C   the impact of fiscal policy on skateboards

   D   the need for more capital investment in their company

Look at the graph below and answer the following question.

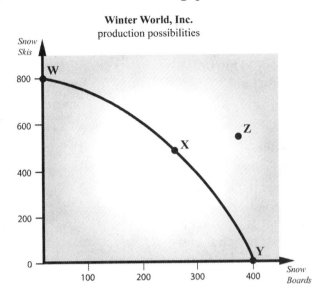

Winter World, Inc.
production possibilities

83 Which of the following points represents the level at which snow skis alone   EF2
could be MOST efficiently produced?

A   W   B   X   C   Y   D   Z

84 Monetary policy MOST affects   MA2

A   the amount of taxes citizens pay.

B   the amount of money government spends.

C   the price of stock in sole proprietorships.

D   interest rates on loans.

85 Which of the following would be   IN2
MOST supportive of British tariffs?

A   A US company hoping to export goods to Great Britain.

B   A British company hoping to export goods to other countries.

C   British consumers.

D   British manufacturers who sell their products domestically.

86 To protect US peanut farmers,   MI3
the federal government sets a
price floor below which the price of
peanuts cannot drop. It also passes a
number of subsidies to help farmers
recover from economic hardship.
Although farmers are glad to get the
relief, these actions will likely result
in

A   the United States becoming a command economy.

B   lower safety standards for peanuts.

C   a surplus of peanuts.

D   a shortage of peanuts.

GO ON

87 Thorndike Corporation has just finished a year of record profits. Rather than use the resources to immediately raise production, they decide to purchase land and materials to build a new plant and purchase updated technology. Thorndike's actions represent what? *EF6*

   A   failure to recognize opportunity costs

   B   capital investment

   C   consumer investment

   D   investment in human capital

88 The idea that what is produced will be determined by what consumers need/want, provided they are willing to pay enough for producers to make a profit, is called what? *MI2*

   A   the market

   B   the law of demand

   C   the law of supply and demand

   D   the influence of disposable income

89 Frank has owned the same Italian bistro in the heart of the city for nearly 23 years. Although it's small, it's known for the best lasagna in town. What kind of business does Frank operate? *EF4*

   A.   sole proprietorship

   B.   partnership

   C.   cooperative

   D.   corporation

90 Susan, Phil, Robert, and Martina are all lawyers. After several years of working for big firms, they decide to pull their resources and start their own law practice together. The four of them will make all their business decisions together and will share all of the profits and financial risk. Their new law firm is a *MI4*

   A   sole proprietorship.

   B   major corporation.

   C   partnership.

   D   franchise.

Georgia US Economics
Practice Test 2

The purpose of this practice test is to measure your progress in US economics. This test is based on the GPS-based EOCT standards for US economics and adheres to the sample question format provided by the Georgia Department of Education.

General Directions:

1. Read all directions carefully.

2. Read each question or sample. Then choose the best answer.

3. Choose only one answer for each question. If you change an answer, be sure to erase your original answer completely.

1 Jake is trying to decide whether **EF1** to take a summer job as a camp counselor or as a farm laborer. The farm labor pays much better, but the work is also much more demanding and he would have less time off. Which of the following could be considered an opportunity cost of taking the job as a farm laborer?

A the higher wage

B the free time that comes with being a counselor

C exposure to noisy angry children

D there is no cost because the wage is higher

2 An economic actor that exists **MI1** primarily to produce a product for a profit is called

A a business or firm.

B a household.

C a government.

D an international organization.

3 Margaret has just received a **PF2** $3000 bonus from work that she was not expecting. Being a very practical person, Margaret does some research and notices that interest rates are currently very high. Because Margaret wants to get as much return from her money as possible, she will be MOST LIKELY to do which of the following?

A She will save her money in a safe at home.

B She will save her money in a bank or investment account.

C She will spend her money while she has enough to pay cash rather than using a credit card.

D She will spend her money and borrow more before interest rates drop.

4 When the Federal Reserve sells **MA2** securities on the open market, it has which of the following effects?

A the money supply increases

B taxes increase

C money supply decreases

D tariffs are put in place

5 Purchasing power parity means **IN3** that—

A $100 will buy the same amount of goods as 100 euros or 100 yen.

B the exchanged value of a currency has the same purchasing power in different countries.

C $100 will buy the same value of foreign currency in any country.

D foreign buyers can buy as much as domestic buyers.

6 Which of following statements **MA1** BEST distinguishes between the terms recession and depression?

A A recession is a period of economic growth, while a depression is a period of economic decline.

B A recession is a period of inflation whereas a depression is a period of deflation

C A depression is longer and more severe than a normal recession.

D A depression affects the households whereas a recession affects businesses and governments.

7 Which of the following is a typi- **EF5** cal role of government in a market economy?

A it owns the majority of land and capital

B price setter

C output setter

D provider of public goods

This table shows the Consumer Price Index figures for the US from 1995–2004 (base year 1984.)

Year	Consumer Price Index (Base Year=1984)
1995	152.5
1996	156.9
1997	160.5
1998	163.0
1999	166.6
2000	172.2
2001	177.1
2002	179.9
2003	184.0
2004	188.9

8   For the years of 1995–2004, the US experienced—   MA1

A   deflation.

B   inflation.

C   both inflation and deflation.

D   neither inflation nor deflation.

9   The fundamental economic   EF4
     questions that all economies
     must answer are

A   who will rule, who will vote, and
     who will pay taxes?

B   what will be produced, how will it
     be produced, and for whom will it
     be produced?

C   who determines the costs, who will
     set the prices, and who determines
     how much is made?

D   how much will be produced, of
     what quality will it be, and who
     will pay for it?

10   Donald purchases $800 in stock   MI4
     in a company called Magnacorp.
     If Magnacorp goes into debt and
     experiences bankruptcy, how much
     will Donald be liable as a partial
     owner in the company?

A   He has unlimited liability and can
     be forced to sell all his tangible
     assets (house, car, etc.) to pay the
     company's debt.

B   He has limited liability and will be
     reimbursed the $800 he invested.

C   He is partially liable to the point
     that he is forced to pay a portion of
     all his future wages/salary until the
     company's debt is paid.

D   He has limited liability and will
     only lose the $800 he invested in
     the company.

GO ON

11 Jack is about to graduate from high school. His parents have saved $45,000 dollars for him. They plan on giving it to him after graduation. Jack has to decide what to do with the money and is torn between buying a new car or paying for college. Which option reflects Jack engaging in a rational decision-making process? **PF1**

A   He immediately goes out to buy the new car.

B   He thinks about the two alternative options, decides what is most important to him, evaluates the alternatives, and makes the rational decision to pay for college with the money.

C   He impulsively decides to pay for half of college and spend the rest on a new car.

D   He does not know what to do with the money so he puts it in the bank.

12 Dalton is part of a household and works for an architecture firm. If the government raises income taxes, Dalton will be MORE LIKELY to **PF3**

A   consume more goods in the market place.

B   consume fewer goods in the market place.

C   invest in more capital.

D   purchase more stock in corporations.

13 A good that is used in place of another good to meet the same need is called a **MI2**

A   complementary good

B   capital good.

C   substitute good.

D   consumer good.

14 Russia and Ukraine are neighboring countries. The table below gives the amount of crude oil and steel that each produces in a day. Which of the statements below is accurate? **IN1**

	Oil	Steel
Russia	8,000	200
Ukraine	80	160

A   Russia has an absolute advantage in oil, and Ukraine has an absolute advantage in steel.

B   Ukraine has a comparative advantage in steel, despite Russia's absolute advantage in both products.

C   Russia and the Ukraine would not benefit from trade because Russia makes both products more cheaply.

D   Ukraine has a comparative advantage in oil, despite the fact that Russia can produce so much more of it.

15 As part of the Central American Free Trade Agreement, the US decides to eliminate all tariffs and quotas on cane sugar. Which of the following actors would be MOST LIKELY to oppose this action? **IN2**

A   makers of SuperSnappy Sugar Crisp cereal in the US

B   US buyers of SuperSnappy Sugar Crisps

C   sugar growers in Louisiana and Texas

D   sugar growers in the Caribbean

16 The act of giving up one thing to obtain another is called **EF1**

A   an opportunity cost.

B   a purchase.

C   a trade-off.

D   an incentive.

17 Which of the following is an investment which allows someone to transfer financial risk? PF5

   A embargoes

   B capital

   C entrepreneurship

   D insurance

18 In the school cafeteria, there are servers, grill cooks, dishwashers, and cash register attendants. Each of these does his/her own specific task. This is a good example of what? EF3

   A full employment

   B mass production

   C arbitration

   D division of labor

19 Which of the following statements BEST differentiates between the terms debt and deficit? MA1

   A Debt and deficit are synonymous (i.e. they have the exact same meaning).

   B Debt means to have more money flowing out than coming in, and deficit is the accumulation of the debt.

   C Deficit means to have more money flowing out than coming in, and debt is the accumulated amount that is owed.

   D Debt and deficit are completely unrelated terms.

20 Fiscal policy is concerned with which of the following? MA3

   A government spending and taxation

   B consumer spending and productivity

   C government spending and the money supply

   D taxation and inflation

21 Dale has a four-year college degree and a master's degree. Olivia has a four-year college degree. Brendan has completed 2 years of college. Margaret has only a high school diploma. Which of the following statements is MOST LIKELY true? PF6

   A Margaret will likely not get a job.

   B Brendan and Margaret have no earning potential.

   C Dale has greater earning potential than Olivia.

   D Dale and Olivia will likely earn less than Margaret.

22 Galen's company has a great year in which they make record profits. Galen decides to use a large percentage of the profits to purchase new, updated equipment. Galen has made what? EF6

   A an investment in human capital

   B a profit maximizing decision

   C a capital investment

   D a decision based on the law of diminishing returns

23 Moses works as a full-time guitarist in a rock and roll band called the "Flaming Whys". Due to a conflict with the lead singer, Moses leaves the band and begins looking for another band in need of a lead guitarist. Which of the following BEST describes the type of unemployment that Moses is experiencing? MA1

   A seasonal

   B cyclical

   C structural

   D frictional

GO ON

24 Teachers and professors buy a lot of books. If changes in the demand for education led to rapidly increasing wages for teachers and professors, how would this affect the price and quantity sold of books? MI2 11

A The price and quantity would rise as teachers' incomes shifted demand to the right.

B The price and quantity would decrease as teachers' incomes shifted demand to the left.

C The price would drop and the quantity would increase as the teachers' incomes shifted supply to the right.

D The price would rise and the quantity would drop as the teachers' incomes shifted supply to the left.

25 In order to make a rational economic decision, one must EF2

A be an entrepreneur.

B understand capital investments.

C be aware of the difference in compound and simple interest.

D be able to assess marginal costs and benefits.

26 After getting a celebrity athlete to endorse its product, Chocobliss Candy Bars finds that consumer taste favors their candy bars because of the star athlete's popularity. As a result of this popularity, what will happen to the supply and price of Chocobliss bars? MI2

A Both will fall.

B Both will rise.

C Supply will rise while price falls.

D Supply will fall while price rises.

27 Emma is a US tourist visiting Niagara Falls. She visits both the US and Canadian sides. Emma wants to buy twenty T-shirts and some other souvenirs. Before traveling, she investigates and finds that, at the current exchange rate of 1 US dollar to 1.25 Canadian dollars, the souvenirs will cost her the same amount on either side of the border. If the exchange rate suddenly shifts to 1 US dollar to 1.5 Canadian dollars, on which side of the border should Emma buy her shirts, and why? IN3

A in Canada because the US dollar has appreciated

B in Canada because the US dollar has depreciated

C in the US because the US dollar has appreciated

D in the US because the US dollar has depreciated

28 Why are interest rates lower for people with collateral? PF4

A These loans have less risk because the borrower has assets that can be taken in place of payment.

B These loans are to people who are less likely to be discriminated against.

C These loans are to people who do not actually need the money.

D These loans are to people who have shown that they are responsible.

29 Increasing the reserve requirement is likely to have which of the following effects? MA2

A increasing the money supply

B decreasing the money supply

C increasing the budget deficit

D decreasing the budget deficit

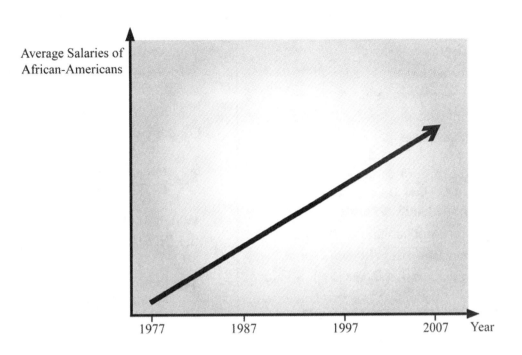

Average Salaries of African-Americans

1977   1987   1997   2007   Year

30 Based on the graph, which of the following would be a safe assumption?   PF6

    A   Fewer African Americans are going to college now than twenty years ago.

    B   African Americans are the most educated population in the United States.

    C   The average earning potential of African Americans has increased in the last three decades.

    D   African Americans, on average, have experienced a decline in earning potential over the last thirty years.

31 Fred receives a loan for $10,000   PF2
that must be repaid in three years. The rate of interest is 5%. If the amount of interest that must be repaid is greater than $1,500, what type of interest is Fred paying?

    A   simple

    B   usury

    C   compound

    D   articulated

32 Which of the following is an   EF5
example of how the US government regulates and/or affects the economy?

    A   inflation

    B   free markets

    C   unrestricted trade

    D   consumer protection policies

GO ON

33 Which of the following would be   PF3
MOST LIKELY to prevent Mar-
cus from taking his family on a vacation to Disney World?

A   lower tariffs

B   rational economic decisions

C   high taxes

D   a decrease in the discount rate

34 Good communication skills, the   PF6
ability to show proper respect,
and knowledge of computers are all

A   forms of capital investment.

B   investments in human capital.

C   qualities that increase one's value
in the labor market.

D   important when making rational
economic choices.

35 When economists monitor the   MA1
state of the economy by keeping
track of changes in the prices of
goods and services typically purchased by consumers, they are using
what economic indicator?

A   gross domestic product

B   per capita gross domestic product

C   stock market

D   consumer price index

36 The flow of goods and services   MI1
from businesses to households
occurs primarily in the

A   factors market

B   intermediary good market

C   product market

D   financial market

37 In a perfectly competitive mar-   MI4
ket, a firm will hire new employees as long as the cost of the added
worker is less than the

A   amount of revenue generated by
the employee.

B   average production cost.

C   amount of physical product generated by the employee.

D   minimum wage set by the Federal
government.

38 Which of the following provides   EF1
the BEST definition of a trade-
off?

A   the act of giving up one thing to
obtain another

B   the value of the best alternative not
chosen

C   the exchange of goods

D   giving up something for an item of
lesser value

39 In market economies, such as   EF4
that of the US, the fundamental
question "how will it be produced?"
is answered by

A   the government.

B   private firms seeking the lowest
cost production method.

C   public firms owned and operated
by the government.

D   consumers' level of demand.

Look at the production possibilities curve below and answer the following question.

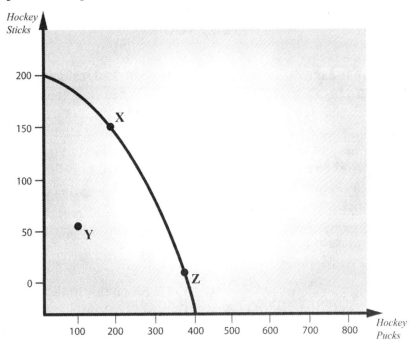

40 **The trade-off of producing hockey sticks at level X is**   EF2

- **A**   200 hockey sticks
- **B**   200 pucks
- **C**   350 pucks
- **D**   150 hockey sticks and 200 pucks

41 **Which of the following is an**   EF6
example of investment in
capital?

- **A**   providing a medical plan to help employees avoid getting sick and missing work
- **B**   providing discount gym memberships to employees to help them stay in shape
- **C**   reinvesting company profits in updated technology
- **D**   paying for employees to get a graduate degree

42 **The government is said to have a**   MA1
balanced budget if

- **A**   the value of imports is equal to the value of exports.
- **B**   tax revenues are up from the previous year.
- **C**   government spending exactly equals the amount of government revenue.
- **D**   both the House of Representatives and the Senate agree on the budget.

Practice Test 2   Session II   Do not begin until your teacher tells you to.

43 The nation of Tupalow is outraged that the Republic of Za has repeatedly violated international human rights laws. As a result, Tupalow decides not to export products to the Republic of Za until that nation shows evidence that it is complying with such laws. Such action is called what?   IN2

   A   a tariff

   B   a trade treaty

   C   an embargo

   D   an unfavorable balance of trade

44 David wants to buy a piece of pizza and go to the movies. However, he only has enough money to do one or the other. In order to decide what to spend his limited money on, David will   PF1

   A   visit a bank.

   B   apply for interest.

   C   hire a financial advisor.

   D   engage in a rational decision-making process.

45 Which of the following statements BEST defines consumer credit?   PF4

   A   to pay for goods in the present for delivery in the future

   B   to pay for goods with something other than cash

   C   to receive goods in the present on agreement that one will pay for them in the future

   D   to buy goods without possessing collateral

46 The Federal government is concerned that economic growth is too high, that it is unsustainable, and that inflation is resulting. Which of the following fiscal policies might be enacted to reduce inflation?   MA3

   A   increasing taxation

   B   open market sales

   C   decreasing taxation

   D   increasing government spending

47 Since the 1980s, the US has   IN3

   A   run high current and capital account deficits.

   B   run high current and capital account surpluses.

   C   run current account surpluses and capital account deficits.

   D   run current account deficits and capital account surpluses.

48 With the advancement of computer technologies, computers were developed that could efficiently operate telephone switching stations. Which of the following would BEST describe the unemployment experienced by people who had previously held jobs as telephone operators?   MA1

   A   structural

   B   frictional

   C   cyclical

   D   seasonal

49 Nigeria and South Africa both produce oil and diamonds. In one day, Nigeria produces 100 units of crude oil and one unit of diamonds. On the other hand, South Africa produces one-half a unit of crude oil and fifty units of diamonds in the same time frame. Which of the following can be accurately said about these two countries? IN1

A Nigeria has a comparative advantage in oil, but South Africa has an absolute advantage in oil.

B Nigeria has a comparative advantage in diamonds, and South Africa has a comparative advantage in oil.

C Nigeria has an absolute advantage in oil, and South Africa has an absolute advantage in diamonds.

D South Africa has a comparative advantage in diamonds, but Nigeria has an absolute advantage in both products.

50 Which of the following is a monetary policy that would be useful in stopping deflation? MA2

A increasing government spending
B decreasing the reserve requirement
C increasing the discount rate
D decreasing taxation

51 Which of the following products is MOST LIKELY to have the lowest level of price elasticity? MI3

A the latest model of a well known sports car
B a successful new cancer medication
C soybeans
D chocolate chip cookies

52 The government would like to increase the money supply. Which of the following might be done to accomplish this task? MA2

A increase the reserve requirement
B increase the discount rate
C buy bonds
D sell bonds

53 If the price of cameras goes down, what will happen to the demand for camera lenses? MI1

A it will decline
B it will increase
C it will be unaffected
D this cannot be known from the available information

54 The value of the BEST alternative that is given up when one makes an economic decision is called the— MI2

A opportunity cost.
B trade-off.
C minimal outcome.
D maximum outcome.

55 The US charges a tax of thirty cents on every dollar's worth of foreign tennis shoes entering the country. Which type of trade barrier is this? IN2

A quota
B non-tariff barrier
C it is not a trade barrier
D tariff

56 Factory machinery is considered to be part of which of the following factors of production? EF1

A capital
B labor
C land
D entrepreneurship

GO ON

57 Amy opens a Web site consulting firm. She faces unlimited liability, but maintains all the decision making authority. What type of business does Amy own? MI4

 A corporation
 B partnership
 C sole-proprietorship
 D franchise

58 US exchange rates are determined entirely by supply and demand. The US, therefore, has a IN3

 A fixed exchange rate
 B floating exchange rate
 C managed floating exchange rate
 D crawling peg exchange rate

59 An economy in which the government owns the means of production and a planning commission determines what gets produced and for whom would BEST be described as a EF4

 A. market economy.
 B. traditional economy.
 C. command economy.
 D. mercantilist economy.

60 The US experienced a recession from March 2001 to November 2001. During this time, companies laid off many employees. Later, many of the employees were rehired when the economy recovered. Which of the following types of unemployment BEST describes this situation? MA1

 A frictional
 B structural
 C cyclical
 D seasonal

61 Which of the following statements BEST distinguishes labor from entrepreneurship? EF1

 A Laborers do physical work and entrepreneurs do mental work.
 B Laborers earn small incomes and entrepreneurs earn large incomes.
 C Laborers work for a living and entrepreneurs earn a return on investments.
 D Laborers earn a wage for their labor and entrepreneurs earn profits for starting a business.

62 The following headline appears in a local paper: "New Product Aims to Attract Teen Girls". Which of the following economic questions does this headline answer? EF4

 A What should be produced?
 B How will it be produced?
 C When will it be produced?
 D For whom will it be produced?

63 Assuming demand remains the same, if the supply of hot dogs is reduced, what will happen to the price of hot dogs? MI2

 A it will increase
 B it will decrease
 C it will remain the same
 D one cannot tell from the information provided

64 Which of the following is a positive occurrence in the US economy? MA1

 A trough
 B contraction
 C expansion
 D depression

65 Bill's business chooses to pro- EF3
duce fluorescent toothbrushes
that allow people to brush their teeth
in the dark because he believes there
is a demand for them. He decided to
embark on this business adventure on
his own, despite some skepticism
from those who know him. Since the
government does not force consumers
to buy what they don't desire, Bill
will have to convince people to purchase his toothbrushes of their own
free will. This scenario is MOSTLY
an example of what?

A a mixed market economy

B a free enterprise system based on
voluntary exchange

C productivity and efficiency

D a corporation at work

66 Country A exports 10% more IN1
goods than it imports. By contrast, country B imports 15% more
goods than it exports. Which of the
following statements is obviously
true?

A Country A has a favorable balance
of trade, but country B has an
unfavorable balance of trade.

B Country A has a comparative
advantage over country B.

C Country B must rely on foreign aid
from country A.

D Country B has a favorable balance
of trade, but country A has an
unfavorable balance of trade.

67 Buying stocks, purchasing PF1
bonds, using profits to buy better machinery, and using part of
one's income to take a training course
are all forms of

A credit.   **C** insurance.

B capital.   **D** investments.

68 Montie needs a loan for school. PF2
After shopping around, he finds
two different institutions offering
school loans at 4.5% interest. North
Rock Bank will finance his education
at 4.5% compounded annually for 5
years after graduation. Meanwhile,
Scholar Tomorrow Funding will
finance Montie's education at 4.5%
simple interest for the same 5 year
period. Finally, Montie gets a credit
card application in the mail that
would allow him to use a credit card
to pay for college at a special rate of
4.3% compounded every 6 months.
Which lender should Montie go with?

A North Rock Bank

B Scholar Tomorrow Funding

C the credit card

D Cannot tell based on the above
information.

69 The fact that the US tends to IN1
import more than it exports,
while at the same time investing less
money in foreign nations than foreign
nations invest in the US is evidence
that

A The US has a capital account
surplus and a current account
deficit.

B The US has a current account surplus and a capital account deficit.

C The US' investments in foreign
nations has created positive net
exports.

D US trade accounts are economically at equilibrium.

GO ON

Use the supply-demand table below to answer question number 67.

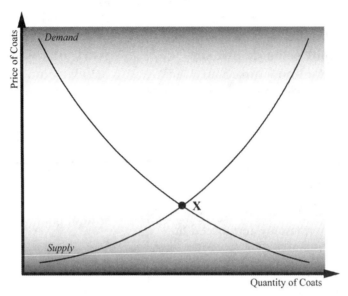

70 **If the demand curve for coats moves left, then supply will**   MI2

   A   increase.

   B   decrease.

   C   remain the same.

   D   it is hard to tell from the available information.

71 **Darren owns his own plumbing**   EF1
business. He spends some of his
company's profits on new pipes and
tools. Jennifer then hires Darren and
his assistant to install a new septic
tank in her back yard. Which of the
following statements is true?

   A   Darren is the consumer.

   B   Jennifer is the investor.

   C   Darren's assistant is an entrepreneur.

   D   The pipes and tools are capital.

72 **Buyers help determine price in a**   MI2
market economy by

   A   how they are taxed.

   B   how much they value the dollar over other forms of currency.

   C   how much they demand a product and are willing to spend.

   D   how much they produce as households.

73 John has been told by his friends PF1 that he makes some awesome t-shirts. John decides that he might want to sell some of them. If John uses the decision-making model and decides that after spending money to buy the shirts and the dye necessary, he can sell the shirts for $1 more than what it cost him to make them, then which of the following statements is true?

A   John won't sell the shirts because his marginal cost is too high.

B   John can make a profit on each shirt, but will likely not sell them because his total cost is higher than the combined total of his variable and fixed costs.

C   John has an incentive to sell the shirts because he stands to make a profit.

D   John has an incentive, but it is unclear whether or not he will make a profit.

74 Jane has worked at the same MA1 factory for over fifteen years. However, yesterday she was called into her supervisor's office and told that she is being laid off because there is a recession and the company cannot afford to employ her until the economy improves. Jane is experiencing

A   economic depression.

B   trough.

C   cyclical unemployment.

D   structural unemployment.

75 Thomas owns an auto dealer- PF3 ship that specializes in selling luxury cars. He reads the morning paper and discovers that the Federal Reserve has just implemented an "easy money" policy. How does Thomas feel about this?

A   He's upset because people will be less likely to buy cars.

B   He's glad because people who can afford it will be more likely to buy cars.

C   He has no opinion because the Fed's actions have nothing to do with the market for cars.

D   He is upset that the Fed's actions may cause a rise in demand.

76 The costs of producing each EF2 additional unit ("just one more") of a particular product is called what?

A   fixed costs

B   marginal costs

C   total costs

D   variable costs

77 In 2007, the United States expe- PF2 rienced record numbers of home foreclosures. In other words, because many people had signed home loans that they ultimately could not afford to pay back, record numbers lost their homes to lenders. Lenders were able to take these homes because the homes were

A   illegally bought.

B   uninsured.

C   collateral.

D   part of a housing surplus.

GO ON

Look at the graph below and answer the following question.

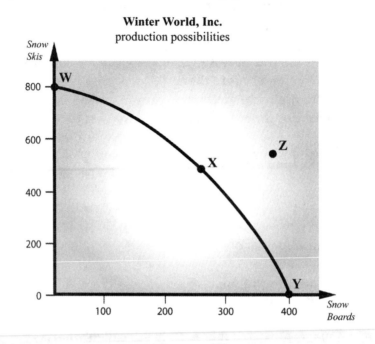

Winter World, Inc.
production possibilities

78 Which of the following points represents a level of production not possible EF2
for snowboards?

A   W   B   X   C   Y   D   Z

79 What role do profits play in a   MI2
market economy?

A   Profits motivate consumers to buy.
B   Profits motivate the government to spend.
C   Profits motivate businesses to produce.
D   Profits motivate the Federal Reserve to lower interest rates.

80 Which of the following is considered a negative side-effect of minimum wage?

A   full employment
B   increased interest rates
C   unemployment
D   failure to meet equilibrium production

81 The study of how individuals, EF1
    firms, and nations can best allo-
    cate their limited resources is called
    what?

    A   entrepreneurship

    B   economics

    C   study of production

    D   capital

82 If a desired item is in such short EF1
    supply that there is not enough
    to meet demand, then that item is said
    to be what?

    A   scarce

    B   rare

    C   renewable

    D   affordable

83 The item mentioned in question EF1
    # 82 will likely be which of the
    following?

    A   cheap

    B   expensive

    C   a renewable natural resource

    D   an opportunity cost

Use the graph below to answer question number 84.

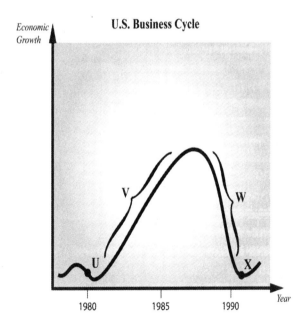

84 Which point on the graph above depicts economic expansion? MA1
    A   U   B   V   C   W   D   X

GO ON

85 The Federal Reserve can best be described as   MA2

A   The most important part of the federal government.

B   The executive branch of government.

C   The key actor in setting fiscal policy.

D   A bank for banks.

86 The island of Mogo is ruled by a king and a council of five elders. The king and this council determine what the islanders need and what can be produced. They also determine at what price things will be sold. Although they allow some people to own private property, they are strict about how such property can be used. It sounds like Mogo has what kind of market?   EF4

A   free-market

B   mixed market that is predominately command

C   command market only

D   true communist market

87 In order for Jamie to paint one additional portrait, it will cost her $50.00. The good news is that, if she paints it, she can probably sell it for $250.00. Which of the following equals Jamie's marginal cost?   EF2

A $50

B $200

C $250

D $300

88 Which of the following MOST resembles a *traditional* economic system?   EF4

A   Susan became a nurse because her mother and grandmother were nurses. Although she could have chosen any profession, she wanted to follow in their footsteps. One day, she plans on returning to medical school and becoming a surgeon.

B   Arthur is a talented man. He is intelligent enough to do almost anything, but the government has assigned him to work in an automobile factory. He hates his job but has no choice since the government makes all economic decisions and stresses the importance of everyone working for the good of the country.

C   Nathan is an excellent cobbler. Because his family has practiced this profession for generations, it is all he ever hoped or was expected to be. The shop he works out of is on land owned by a wealthy landlord and, although he takes great pride in his work, Nathan will likely never advance beyond where he currently is in life.

D   Paula has pulled herself up by the bootstraps. Although she was born poor, she worked hard in school and earned a scholarship. She graduated with honors and now works for a large corporation. Taking advantage of the opportunities afforded her, she was able to buy her parents a new house and send her baby brother to college as well.

Use the graph below to answer question number 89.

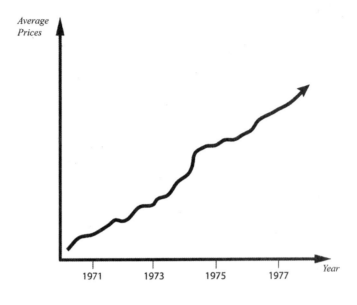

89 What does the graph above MOST LIKELY depict?   MA1

    A   GDP
    B   trade balances
    C   interest rates
    D   CPI

90 **When trying to make a rational**   EF2
    economic decision one would
    need to consider which of the follow-
    ing?

    A   factors of production
    B   the impact of government subsi-
         dies
    C   potential opportunity costs
    D   net exports

M

managed floating exchange rate, 85
market economy, 27
medium of exchange, 39
minimum wage, 45
mixed economies, 29
monetary policy, 66
money, 39
monopoly, 48
mutual funds, 98

N

national debt, 56
natural resources, 17
needs, 17
nonrenewable natural resources, 17
North American Free Trade Agreement (NAFTA), 82

O

oligopoly, 48
open market operations, 68
opportunity cost, 22

P

partnership, 49
peak, 64
price ceilings, 45
price floors, 45
principal, 107
product market, 38
productivity, 24, 88
productivity and efficiency, 25
proprietorship, 49
prosperity, 64
purchasing power, 88
purchasing power parity, 88

Q

quantity demanded, 42
quota, 76

R

recession, 64
recovery, 64
renewable natural resources, 17
re-possess, 108
resources, 17

S

savings and loan associations, 97
scarcity, 19
seasonal unemployment, 60
sellers, 46
shareholders, 50
shortage, 42

simple interest, 107
sole proprietorship, 49
specialization, 24
stock market, 50
stocks, 50, 98
structural unemployment, 59
subsidy, 78
substitute goods, 44
supply, 40
supply and demand, law of, 40
supply curve (or supply schedule), 41
surplus, 42

T

tariffs, 76
trade-off, 22
traditional economies, 26
trough, 64

U

unemployment
    cyclical, 58
    frictional, 59
    rate, 58
    seasonal, 60
    structural, 58
United Nations (UN), 82
unlimited liability, 49
unlimited life, 50

V

voluntary exchange, 24

W

wage and price controls, 45
wages, 37
wants, 17
wants and/or needs, 19
World Trade Organization (WTO), 81